➤WHAT DOES IT TAKE TO RAISE A *MODERN-DAY* SPIRITUAL CHAMPION?

If you're like most parents, you think you're doing an okay job—and you probably believe you're doing better than most. But if your goal is to raise kids with a life-impacting faith, that may not be good enough.

Determined to learn the secrets of those who've raised spiritual champions, world-renowned researcher George Barna conducted a series of surveys and thousands of personal interviews with both young adults and their parents.

In the process, he was able to uncover a number of common denominators to parenting success. Some of his findings will encourage you; others will surprise you. But be forewarned—raising a spiritual champion takes Revolutionary Parenting.

Visit Tyndale's exciting Web site at www.tyndale.com.

TYNDALE and Tyndale's quill logo are registered trademarks of Tyndale House Publishers, Inc.

Barna and the Barna logo are trademarks of George Barna.

BarnaBooks is an imprint of Tyndale House Publishers, Inc.

Revolutionary Parenting: Raising Your Kids to Become Spiritual Champions

Designed by Stephen Vosloo

Edited by Anita K. Palmer

The Library of Congress has catalogued the hardcover edition as follows:

Barna, George.
Revolutionary parenting : what the research shows really works / George Barna.
p. cm.
Includes bibliographical references.
ISBN 978-1-4143-0760-2 (hc)
1. Parenting—Religious aspects—Christianity. 2. Child rearing—Religious aspects—Christianity. I. Title.
BV4529.B368 2007
248.8′45—dc22 2006037354

ISBN 978-1-4143-3937-5 (sc)

Printed in the United States of America

16 15 14 13 12 11 10
7 6 5 4 3 2

This book is dedicated to George and Constance Barna, my parents. Your hard work and sacrifices produced a child who loves God with all his heart, mind, strength, and soul. Thanks for your devotion to being great parents.

➤contents

acknowledgments

THIS BOOK HAS BEEN a long time in the making and a major matter of prayer for many of us. Let me briefly thank those who played a significant role in the process.

At The Barna Group, Yuly Magana and Pam Jacob were instrumental in the information-gathering and editing processes. David Kinnaman and Cameron Hubiak held the company together, and Celeste Rivera kept customers and clients happy while I went off to write. They are a competent and special team.

My colleague at The Barna Group and at Good News Holdings, Thom Black, was helpful in facilitating the publication of the book through Tyndale House.

My friends at Tyndale House have been patient, encouraging, and professional in dealing with this project. Special thanks go to Jan Long Harris, Doug Knox, Sharon Leavitt, and Caleb Sjogren, the front-line players of the team that has guided and supported me through the process.

As usual, my family was very understanding as I locked myself in the dungeon and pounded out the manuscript. My wife, Nancy, has been particularly gracious during the time spent developing this resource. My daughters—Samantha, Corban, and Christine—have been steadfast in praying for me and this book, and have been very understanding regarding my absentmindedness during the writing period. I pray that some of the wisdom gleaned from this project will help Nancy and me to be Revolutionary Parents.

I had many people praying for me during this venture. Among my prayer partners have been Bill and Jacki Dahl, Traver Dougherty, Bill and Lorraine Frey, Gary and Catherine Greig, Stephan Joubert, Paul Lewis, Dan McGowan, Gary Rosberg, Steve Russo, Tim Smith, Tim Tassapoulos, Brett White, and my friends at the International Network of Children's Ministry.

Finally, I am indebted to the thousands of people we interviewed for this project, and especially to those whom we interviewed multiple times. While I cannot thank each of you by name, "you know who you are." I hope this book reflects the wisdom you so generously passed along for me to share with others.

May God, for whose glory and purposes this book was written, be blessed by this effort and by any positive transformation that it stimulates.

TALK ABOUT PRODUCT OVERLOAD.

Did you know that if you took all of the books available today on parenting and divided them by the number of days in a year, you'd discover that there has been an average of ten new parenting books produced every day of the year for each of the past twenty-one years? That's more than 75,000 different parenting books currently at your disposal. That sure seems like overkill, don't you think?

On the other hand, you can argue that such a vast quantity of parenting books would not have been produced unless there was a market for them. While few of those publications have reached best-seller status, we might safely assume that enough of them have been profitable to entice publishers to continue releasing new titles in this category.

But why, with the glut of such books—some of which have penetrated deeply into our culture—do we need yet another take on parenting?

That's a great question—and one that I struggled with for a long time while pondering the offer to write this book.

FIVE POPULAR CATEGORIES

En route to arriving at a satisfactory answer, I examined the titles and subtitles of the hundred best-selling books on parenting. You know, you can get a pretty good idea of the content of parenting books simply by exegeting the titles! The experts writing these hundred books, I learned, suggest that good parenting—or, at least, survival as a parent—encompasses five dimensions.

According to these experts, a great parent needs certain *personal attributes*, such as patience, love, a positive attitude, and self-confidence. Secondly, some of the popular volumes spell out *imperative parental practices*, describing the importance of playing with children; establishing parental authority and control; meting out discipline and punishment; resolving conflict with the child; developing an emotional connection; utilizing drugs and vaccinations to foster physical and mental health; and praying together. A third category says mandatory *parenting philosophy and perspectives* include coming to peace with one's own past as well as knowing how to plan for effective parenting. Some of the requisite *child-rearing skills*, a fourth category, include the use of logic, creating efficient developmental systems, communicating effectively, and being well-organized. And last, what parent doesn't want to produce *tangible outcomes* in the child's life? The hot books suggest that such results include articulation, generosity, contentment, independence, a love of learning, physical fitness, and cultural sensitivity.

Doesn't it make you tired just reciting everything the experts say you must master?

But my exploration of what has been written about parenting—yes, I did dig beneath the titles—identified a significant weakness in the literature. Virtually every book is based upon personal observations, experiences, or assumptions. Very little of the content is based on objective, projectable research.

NO EVIDENCE DEMANDED

Most of these guides promote a particular point of view or parenting strategy, even though that approach has not been empirically tested or validated through some type of scientific process. Many of these authors are smart people, but by sharing their personal experience—and pretty much basing their exhortations on that limited scope of reality—here's what we get: *the isolated leading the desperate*.

For instance, parenting books typically ignore the *motivation* for engaging in parenting. The implied motivation is that parents should raise their child simply because the child exists and the parents are responsible for that reality. There is rarely any recognition of the fact that the child is a special gift and that raising children is a responsibility assigned to parents by God. As such, parenting bears an innate importance and an irrefutable connection to parenting principles furnished by God.

Another example: Few books acknowledge that God has designed every human being as a unique individual, eliminating the possibility of effective one-size-fits-all parenting strategies. While it is a natural temptation to want a standardized checklist of actions that produces predictably favorable results, the individuality of each person suggests that such a simple tool is not likely to be effective.

Another distinctive of many parenting books is that they offer advice without much relationship to the real-world results their advice generates. Many of the books I've examined recommend strategies that may be innovative but are disconnected from any evidence that their approach produces desirable development in a young person.

Perhaps authors don't produce evidence because it's not demanded of them. Parents, faced with three dominant models (described below) competing for their acceptance, just are too busy to bother. Each of these alternatives has its own appeal and weaknesses.

COMPETING MODELS

One unavoidable influence on parenting behavior is that of societal norms, traditions, and expectations. Because we live within the context of these forces, they have a powerful impact on what we perceive effective parenting to be. Many of these cultural factors are low profile or practically invisible; we practice them simply because we see or experience these elements so frequently in the media or in our daily excursions. Adopting the parenting habits and patterns driven by cultural forces might be described as *parenting by default*.

The second set of influences that shapes our parenting choices and behaviors is that derived from personal experience and outcomes. Doing what comes naturally or what we've learned from past endeavors, we raise children in relation to the insights gleaned in the trenches. This trial-and-error process might be considered *experimental parenting*.

The third approach available to parents, which creates the greatest emotional tension in the parenting marketplace of ideas and practices, comes from the application of biblical commands, principles, and narratives. In this parenting model, God's Word provides the perspective and the marching orders on how to raise a young person. The goal of such child rearing is to raise children who make their faith in God, and relationship with Him, their highest priority in life, and proceed to live as intentional and devoted servants of God. The role of parents is to guide the child to understand the principles and outcomes that honor God and advance His purposes. Success in this venture is measured by transformed lives. I have labeled this one *Revolutionary Parenting*.

I bet you can guess which of the three I am promoting.

Our research conducted for this book indicates that few parents are purists—that is, few parents draw only from the well of standards and practices associated with just one of those three platforms. Most American parents concoct their own unique mixture of parenting ideas and routines, based on a rather general idea of what they are seeking to achieve. The research suggests that most parents talk a better parenting game than they play, largely because they have such vague notions about the process and product. Yet the research also reveals that it is possible to perform one's parenting functions at a very high level of personal competence and productivity—if a particular set of parameters are in place. We'll get to those.

So to get back to our earlier question: Do we need another parenting book? I believe the answer is yes.

TOWARD SPIRITUAL CHAMPIONS

A good researcher identifies the assumptions and hypotheses underlying his study because those elements invariably shape the nature and outcomes of the research. Here's how

I studied the practices of those who have successfully raised spiritual champions.

In 2003 I wrote *Transforming Children into Spiritual Champions* almost by mistake. It was an attempt to discover what Christian churches were doing that was effective in helping children become serious followers of Jesus Christ. It became a surprise best seller and has apparently helped tens of thousands of churches to understand that people's lives are shaped primarily when they are very young, making ministry to children the single most influential ministry any church engages in.

By spiritual champions, I mean individuals who have embraced Jesus Christ as their Savior and Lord; accept the Bible as truth and as the guide for life; and seek to live in obedience to its principles and in search of ways to continually deepen their relationship with God. Spiritual champions live in ways that are noticeably different from the norm—even when compared to the average churchgoer.

For instance, they possess a biblical worldview that shapes their decision-making process because they accept scriptural principles as true and significant. As an integral part of that worldview, they contend that there are moral absolutes that are relevant to our lives and have dramatic consequences if compromised. They believe that they have been created by God to serve Him in specific ways; acknowledge the continual spiritual war between God and Satan in which both of those supernatural powers can influence their choices; and believe that our lives should reflect the character of God. Spiritual champions donate unusually generous amounts of time and money to spiritually driven causes. They carefully screen the media they ingest and have a deep and intense commitment to their relationship with God and other Christians. On a daily basis they strive to change the world in small but life-impacting ways, whether it is done through feeding the hungry, counseling the bereaved, encouraging the confused, protecting the environment, or other means.

In the context of current American life, spiritual champions lead a Revolutionary existence. Their life perspectives are uncommon, their relationships are unique, and their emphasis on the centrality of their faith in God is stunning. Without a doubt, their lives are the product of unusual but intentional preparation.

But one of the lessons that emerged from the research on which my earlier book was based was that churches alone do not and cannot have much influence on children. In fact, the greatest influence a church may have in affecting children is by impacting their parents.

The facts have been indisputably clear: In assessing the impact of churches, schools, and parents, it is the latter who have the most dramatic personal influence on a child. Yet we also learned that most parents are not prepared to be effective in their roles. They often lack the self-confidence needed to fully invest themselves in the process. Consequently, they seek individuals and organizations to help them handle the burden of shaping their child's life in positive ways.

Remember all those parenting books I alluded to earlier?

They haven't helped much. The typical American parents—even after taking in parenting books and articles, workshops, radio programs, and countless conversations—remain stymied as to how to succeed. They are all too happy to pass off their kids to paid professionals—teachers, pastors, babysitters, and coaches.

KEY ASSUMPTIONS

So we crafted a discovery process whose results were intended to help the average parent make the most of his or her window of opportunity.

Our assumptions were simple:

- First, it is important to raise children to know, love, and serve God with all their hearts, minds, strength, and souls. We are spiritual people and must be raised with our spiritual needs and potential in mind.
- Second, parents do not have complete control of the shaping of their children, but they do have substantial influence on who the children become.
- Third, there are undoubtedly some common factors that are pertinent to the child-rearing efforts of parents who successfully raise children to become spiritual champions.

Our objective was to amass a body of knowledge that could be absorbed and applied by all parents who are comfortable with my assumptions to help them maximize their parenting potential.

THE RESEARCH PROCESS

To reach the goals I established for this book, The Barna Group embarked on several distinct but interrelated lines of nationwide, projectable research.

First, we conducted a series of national public-opinion surveys related to parenting experiences and observations. These were nationwide telephone surveys among parents of children under eighteen, in which we inquired about the challenges, successes, and failures of parents.

Second, we explored the existing literature on parenting practices, particularly those works related to incorporating a significant spiritual dimension into the process. This provided us with various elements thought to be of significance in raising children to be faith Revolutionaries.[1] Related primary research then delved into those factors more deeply to examine them more fully.

The third aspect of our research was to comb through more than ten thousand personal interviews we had conducted during the past several years to identify people in their twenties who were leading "transformed" lives. To us, living a transformed life meant more than simply being religious or active in a church.[2] We wanted young adults whose faith was robust: In addition to being active in church life, they were engaged in spiritual activities apart from the control or management of their churches, and they had significant personal faith lives that were mature and still in active development. We created standards related to behavior and belief in the areas of corporate and personal faith. The goal, of course, was to find out what had happened during their formative years that led them to become irrepressible followers of Christ.

We then interviewed these people again, using a long, highly focused questionnaire to glean insights into their upbringing. After we completed each interview we asked for permission to speak to their parents. The intention was to have the parents of these transformed young people describe what they believed they had done that resulted in the emergence of a devoted and mature follower of Christ.

By conducting research among these two generations—the change agent and the changed agent, if you will—we had access to two unique perspectives on the parenting process. As it turned out, there was tremendous consistency between what the parents said they did and what their spiritually transformed children remembered experiencing.

BRAKES ON THE PROCESS

After it was completed, the research went untouched for about a year. There were several reasons for this. First, the sheer volume of books already written on parenting—their previously noted weaknesses notwithstanding—diminished my sense of urgency to add one more tome to the list.

Second, I was reluctant to cast myself in the role of "parenting expert." The research would provide a unique angle on what might increase the odds of growing a spiritual giant, but the thought of being perceived as someone who had the magic formula for producing such a child was personally uncomfortable.

Third, that discomfort was magnified by some parenting issues that arose with my own children while I wrestled with the viability of converting the research findings into a book. If I was already struggling with the idea of being seen as an "expert parent," my obvious failings in certain situations with my daughters seemed to verify my lack of qualifications for writing this book.

Finally, my preliminary analysis of the findings showed that there would be no easy, five-step formula to emerge from this work. Knowing that Americans want quick, simple answers to complex questions, I felt that the research might not gain a fair hearing from the public for whom it was intended. Never one to waste personal resources on dubious ventures, I figured this project might not deserve the investment of energy and other resources necessary to generate such a book.

But, as you can tell (since you're holding this book in your hands), something happened to trump all of those objections.

EQUIPPING THE FRONT LINE

It started with a sense that the Kingdom of God would be better served by the presence of this book than by its absence. Why? Because parenting occurs on the front lines of the spiritual battle that defines our daily existence and purpose.

Thanks to my research related to child development and spiritual growth, I have become convinced that the spiritual war occurring in individual lives is pretty much won or lost by the age of thirteen. What parents do with their youngsters prior to the teen years is of paramount importance to the

Kingdom of God on earth. Not to get dramatic, but I sensed an obligation to offer even a minute amount of assistance to the beleaguered parents of our country.

A second motivation was the unsolicited interest in such a book coming from the spiritual Revolutionaries. My book *Revolution* hit a nerve among tens of thousands of people. Some people's response was to see if I could be deported. (Okay, not quite, but it seemed like that was the way some folks reacted.) Others, however, resonated with the theme of that book and wanted to know how to nurture such an intense, full-speed-ahead faith in Christ in their children's lives. This research certainly addressed their issues and would meet an expressed need.

I decided I should simply do my best to be an obedient and responsible servant of God by fulfilling my calling as a leader, writer, and researcher. As always, if I am being faithful to the calling, then the results are up to God.

WHAT'S COMING UP

In part 1 ("Reasons"), I describe the crisis in American parenting. Most parents are focused on the wrong standards of success and are willing either to settle for what their well-intentioned but ill-informed efforts produce or to deny that there is any problem to address. As a result, our children are suffering in various dimensions of life, but especially in the spiritual dimension. This crisis is seriously undermining the potential of our next generation to become spiritual champions.

In part 2 ("Research"), you will be exposed to survey data,

qualitative information from our in-depth interviews with parents, biblical passages, and interpretive prose. Together we will explore the conditions, priorities, thought processes, values, lifestyles, spiritual thrusts, objectives, and philosophies of parents who have raised spiritual champions. Throughout the book, these child-rearing stalwarts will be referred to as Revolutionary Parents.

In part 3 ("Relevance"), you'll find a summary of what the Bible says about parents, as well as a personal look at how one father made some changes based on this research.

You need to know from the beginning that I won't be offering a simple game plan to follow if you, too, want to produce children who mature into twenty-first-century disciples of Jesus. But I do believe that this book contains some of the pieces to the puzzle that will guide your journey toward raising spiritual champions. I learned that every one of the Revolutionary Parents pieced the puzzle together differently; you will have to do so, too. But knowing the pieces, and what the puzzle might look like in the end, is itself valuable as we seek to honor God and advance His Kingdom through our efforts to raise our children.

➤ part one REASONS

chapter one

A CRISIS IN AMERICAN PARENTING

PARENTING IS HARD work with no guarantees. You probably know people you respect whose efforts in raising their children you have admired—only to find out later that their children did not turn out as expected. Likewise, you may have read some of the acclaimed manuals on how to be an influential parent, only to find that the advice dispensed did not produce the desired outcomes.

This parenting stuff is tricky business. What makes it especially difficult is that the rest of our lives do not stop in the midst of these efforts, enabling us to give our undivided attention and full energy to raising our children. Sadly, helping our kids develop is just one of the tasks in the plethora of responsibilities we juggle every day.

What makes this task most difficult, though, is that for those of us who have decided to follow Christ as our only hope for gaining truth, purpose, direction, and eternal security, there is no obligation that has greater significance than parenting.

None.

If you're like most parents, you feel you're doing an okay job, based on your own standards—and you're likely to believe that you're certainly doing better than most other parents in the country. You do what you can to provide the best for your young ones. You can't be criticized for not trying: You work hard, you provide a good life for your kids, and you are committed to providing them with what you had growing up and more. You involve the kids in a variety of activities, monitor their whereabouts, and take care of their health. Nobody can accuse you of being a slug when it comes to parenting.

As you examine the state of the nation, you recognize that many—maybe even most—children are not as fortunate as yours. Most kids do not have parents who love them and take care of them like you do yours. Most children do not conduct themselves as well as yours. And most children do not have the exposure to religious training that yours receive in church and through other programs and events.

YOU GET WHAT YOU MEASURE

Our conclusions are based upon the criteria we have adopted for the assessment of our children's well-being. Think about it. What do we seek to provide for our children? We want them to be happy, safe, comfortable, good citizens, educated, religious, and fulfilling their potential. The criteria parents use to determine the condition of their children are substantial. Most parents would examine the state of their children and conclude they are:

- Provided with their basic needs: food, clothing, shelter
- Physically healthy
- Performing at or beyond their grade level
- In a secure and comfortable home
- Monitored and cared for by parents
- Involved with church services and programs
- Connected to decent friends
- Not involved in gangs
- Not taking drugs
- Not alcoholics
- Not out-of-control sexually
- Not involved in a cult or in satanic activity
- Not the victim of physical or emotional abuse
- Without a criminal record or related problems

These measures are meaningful—as far as they go. But here's the invisible problem that hampers the development of America's children: We are measuring their well-being based upon the wrong standards. Without realizing it, we have made *ourselves* the judge and jury of what is right and wrong, good and bad, useful and useless in relation to our children's lives.

You are not likely to get the right outcome if you base your actions on the assessment of the wrong things. Yet when it comes to raising our children, Americans have created a matrix of measurements based upon what our society defines to be significant. We gather the raw data for those indices based upon the best information we are able to capture from the ever-present, omniscient mass media. We analyze what we learn based upon our standards and make corrections as needed. The result, of course, is that our children are constantly receiving "the best care" available.

Think about that process for a moment. We have replaced God with ourselves, usurping leadership over our children's circumstances. We have ignored God's Word when it comes to determining how well we're doing, believing that if our conditions meet the social norms, we're most likely in compliance with God's expectations. And we make our judgments and comparisons on the basis of the popular wisdom and criteria dispensed by a mass media that is run for profit by groups of people who have no intention or desire of pleasing God or meeting His standards through the material they produce and distribute. With that in mind, it would not be hard to challenge some of the common thinking about the "okayness" of our children.

For instance, we could note the decline in educational performance: Reading skills are declining, writing skills are abysmal, math ability is below par, and science knowledge is lacking. We could expose the percentages of teens and adolescents having sexual intercourse, smoking, drinking, using drugs, or being victimized by violent crime. Some of the rates of activity in these areas have declined in recent years, but millions and millions of our children remain caught up in such lifestyles. We could harp on the 13 million children who live in poverty, or the 18 million who are being raised by a single parent. We could highlight the issue of physical health, focusing on the 12 million children who are overweight, or the millions of children (particularly girls) who wrestle with anorexia and bulimia, or the 8 million children who receive subpar health care because they have no health insurance.[1]

But that would be missing the point, too.

WHAT DOES GOD MEASURE?

What *is* the point? That God is the absolute judge of how well our children are doing, that His standards examine the character and faith of our young people, and His ways are often not facilitated by many of the activities we promote or endorse, regardless of our ignorance or good intentions.

You get what you measure. If you want intellectuals, measure their exposure to complex information and ideas, and their performance on sophisticated tests. If you want great athletes, evaluate how committed they are to advanced physical training and how superbly they perform in sporting competitions. If you want relational people, determine how connected and popular they are among their peers.

What does God measure? Our hearts. He created us to love, serve, and obey Him.[2] So He studies the indicators of our devotion to Him. As parents, then, our job is to raise spiritual champions. That does not mean we are supposed to ignore the significance of developing our children's intellectual, emotional, and physical dimensions. But it suggests that we have to see the bigger picture of God's priorities and raise our children in light of His standards, not ours or society's.

FAILING BY GOD'S STANDARDS

If we were to gauge how well we're doing in this regard, the outcomes might startle you. Consider these findings from a recent survey we conducted among a nationally representative sample of children between the ages of eight and twelve.[3]

- Most of our children are biblically illiterate, which will become clear as you read on. Their ignorance of Bible teachings corresponds to the fact that only one-third (36 percent) of our adolescents fully believe that the Bible is accurate in all of the principles it teaches.
- Few of our children are motivated to share their faith in Christ with others. Less than one out of every five (19 percent) contend that they have a responsibility to evangelize their peers.
- Not even half of our young people (46 percent) state that their religious faith is very important in their lives.
- Few of our children take Satan seriously. Only one-fourth of them (28 percent) completely dismiss the idea that Satan is symbolic, instead believing that the devil is real.
- Salvation baffles most of our young ones. Only two out of every ten reject the idea that good people can earn their way into heaven. And only three out of every ten dismiss the belief that everyone experiences the same postdeath outcome, regardless of their beliefs. In fact, only two out of every ten adolescents (21 percent) strongly disagree with the statement that people cannot know for sure what will happen to them after they die.

- Most of our kids are willing to entertain the idea that Jesus Christ sinned while He lived on earth. Only 44 percent outright dismiss the idea.
- The majority live for things other than loving God with all their hearts, minds, strength, and souls. Specifically, only four out of ten live with that purpose in mind.
- Three out of four young people reject the notion that there is no such thing as God. However, not only is that lower than expected based upon adult surveys, but we found that fewer young people today—only 58 percent—believe that God is the all-knowing, all-powerful Creator of the universe who still rules His creation. That result is lower than any we have seen in the last quarter century of survey work. A similar percentage (about six out of every ten) believes that God originally created the universe.
- Only one-third of America's adolescents ardently contend that Jesus Christ returned to physical life after His crucifixion and death on the cross.
- By their own admission, our children are confused theologically. Based on their reaction to statements like "It doesn't matter what religious faith I follow because they all teach similar lessons," it's clear that they do not know what to think about competing worldviews and belief systems.

Add to this last fact that our national surveys of thirteen-year-olds reveal that most of them think they already know everything of significance in the Bible (hence, they are no longer open to learning or actively studying the Scriptures). Also, most of them have no intention of continuing to attend a church when they are in their twenties and living on their own.[4]

In addition, consider that fewer than one out of every five parents of young children believe they are doing a good job of training their children morally and spiritually. In fact, when we asked a national sample of adults with children under eighteen to rate their parenting performance on fifteen different indicators, we discovered that parents ranked their efforts related to morality and spirituality at the bottom of the list.

What does all of this add up to? A crisis.

For a host of reasons, we are failing to train children to become the spiritual champions that God created them to be.

SOLVING THE PROBLEM

So how do we address this crisis?

Our natural inclination would be to do one of two things. The most common reaction, according to our studies, is for parents to deny that the problem is as bad as the data suggest.

Americans have a tendency to repudiate facts that discredit what they believe to be true. In more than two decades of research regarding America's faith and lifestyles, we have seen this inclination emerge over and over again. The more sensitive people are to the criticism raised, the more likely their initial reaction will be to reject the facts of the argument, if not the argument itself.

The second common reaction is to push the problem

onto someone else. When it comes to the well-being of their children, people might naturally turn such matters over to the government, local schools, or perhaps churches to make things right.

In this case, however, governments are running scared from addressing overtly religious issues, defending themselves against lawsuits for allegedly corrupting the balance between church and state. Schools, as wards of the state, struggle with similar limitations. Conventional churches, which are generally sympathetic to the crisis, are partly responsible for the spiritual problems we've identified, and most of them are in no position—practically or biblically—to provide a solution.

These responses to reality are the catalysts to ineffective parenting. In the introduction, I referred to three styles of parenting: among them were *parenting by default* and *experimental parenting*. Those approaches are driven by the inability to wisely and strategically address the facts. The ones who suffer the most from parental inefficacy are the children.

A JOB FOR PARENTS

Fortunately, the fact that neither government nor schools are the solution to the problem is not a big deal. That's because they are not the ones responsible for fixing the problem.

The responsibility for raising spiritual champions, according to the Bible, belongs to parents. The spiritual nurture of children is supposed to take place in the home. Organizations and people from outside the home might support those efforts, but the responsibility is squarely laid at the feet of the family. This is not a job for specialists. It is a job for parents.

Recalling the pressures and challenges already burdening most parents, how then can this demanding task be accomplished?

That's the reason for this book. Based upon a nationwide study of children who grew up to be spiritual champions and the parents who raised them that way, we will explore the process that seems to facilitate the emergence of young people who have become fully developed human beings—in the spiritual, physical, emotional, and intellectual dimensions.

The information learned about this process may not make it any easier to be a parent, but it is sure to make it a more focused and productive experience.

part two RESEARCH

CONDITIONS FOR REVOLUTIONARY SUCCESS

MOST PARENTS WANT to do a great job of raising their kids. However, possessing such a laudable desire is what social scientists would call a "necessary but insufficient condition" required to succeed in that task. Transforming a helpless infant into a godly adult is a challenging and consuming endeavor. The most unnerving reality is that even when a parent does everything "right," there is no guarantee that the result will be an adult who honors God with all his or her heart, mind, strength, and soul. Successful parenting is undoubtedly one of the most daunting endeavors any human being can embrace.

Thankfully, some relief is found in the Bible. God tells us that if we have surrendered our lives to Him and are listening for His guidance (through the Bible, other believers, and the Holy Spirit), then we may give Him and our children the best effort we can muster and confidently leave the results to

Him. The Scriptures remind us that while we have free will, we do not possess control over reality.

Nothing drives that point home harder than our experience raising children. Our job is not to succeed but to be obedient to God's calling and principles and allow Him to produce the outcomes according to His perfect will.

With that in mind, perhaps we can take a deep breath and relax. As much as you love your children, God loves them more. As deeply as you desire to do what is best for your children, God wants it even more urgently. As we rely upon Him rather than our own ideas and wisdom, we can be assured that our young ones will experience the best that God has to offer, through us and others.

However, our research also shows that once we allow God to be the mastermind behind our parenting endeavors, there are steps we can take and practices we can implement that boost our capacity to partner with God in raising a spiritual champion.

One thing we can do is foster specific conditions that increase the probability of our children becoming all that God intends them to be. Let's identify those conditions.

A COACHING MODEL OF PARENTING

Have you ever thought of yourself as your child's coach? That is essentially what you are. Coaches take the raw material they are handed, define success, and attempt to shape the individuals being coached into topflight performers.

Every champion needs a qualified coach. Every team in

the World Series or Super Bowl comes with a complement of specialized coaches. The amateur athletes competing at the Olympics come with their coach in tow, often at great expense to their families.

The idea of coaching is consistent with the biblical notion that we are not complete and perfect on our own; we need the assistance of wise mentors and a community of people who care about us.

Successful coaches are an interesting and varied lot. Some who have reached the upper echelon of success in the sports world are former champions—but most of them are not. All of them, though, understand what it takes to become a champion; all of them are committed to helping their protégés ascend to the highest levels of performance; and all of them energetically reinforce championship-caliber efforts.

We acknowledge the importance of having a coach for skills related to sports, academics, music, art, leadership, business, and physical conditioning. How much more important is it for us to ensure that we, as parents, become the ultimate coaches for our children as they develop into mature human beings? There is no dimension more important than their spiritual nature. If you do not accept your God-given responsibility to raise your children to be spiritual champions, how do you expect such a transformation to happen?

Great coaches start with a clear notion of the outcomes they want their protégés to achieve and view them through that lens. Whether in the realm of athletics, academics, or business or personal life, the coach's outcomes are very specific. For instance, the goal might be to lead the team to the national championship; prepare a student to achieve a 4.0 grade point average; enable a CEO to make decisions that guide her corporation to increase profits by 5 percent; or help a person lose twenty pounds in five weeks. Having a clear handle on the desired results is the first step toward achieving that product.

So perhaps we have reached an in-your-face challenge to your parenting: What specific outcomes are you committed to facilitating in your child's life? We'll talk more about them, but a coach-parent who lacks clear goals for his or her child is not likely to achieve desirable results.

Of course, all great coaches have a love for the outcomes they are striving to inspire others to reach. Becoming a champion, in any dimension of life, is a grueling process; you must have a true thirst for the desired outcome. That is certainly true regarding the spiritual development of a child. You cannot hope to raise a spiritual champion unless *you* love God with all your heart, mind, strength, and soul. That commitment must be clearly seen through your life before you can hope to have children who embrace that objective. And they must see you investing in your own spiritual growth before they will accept the importance of their personal commitment to becoming a genuine disciple of Jesus Christ. Anything less will strike them as hypocrisy—and undermine your efforts to move them to higher planes of maturity.

You want to be the best parent you can be for your child—you would not bother reading this book otherwise. But if successful parenting demands that you be a great coach, what exactly does a great coach do?

Here are five tips gleaned from studying parents who have raised godly young adults.

1. *Your impact on your children's lives is proportional to the depth of the relationship you have fostered with them.* Your ability to influence your children is dependent upon them respecting you and trusting you. Expecting them to do what you say simply because you are their parent doesn't work for long. Unless you have gained their attention and favor by becoming a genuine confidant, they eventually will opt for other alternatives.

   You build such trust by showing them unconditional love, complete integrity, and total commitment to the ways of God and their best interests. This implies devoting substantial amounts of time to building your relationship with each child. (Our research underscores the silliness of the "quality time" argument; there is no substitute for investing substantial time in your relationship with your children.) Further, you gain their respect by exhibiting clarity about what you believe and by consistently and unapologetically modeling those principles. Once you have created a true relationship with them, they will be open to your guidance, even when it seems counterintuitive, exceedingly difficult, or out of step with cultural norms.

   A coach who lacks a relationship with a protégé has little chance of convincing that person to take big risks, work hard, or sacrifice immediate personal gain for a greater good.

2. *You must wholeheartedly embrace the outcomes you are pushing the child to achieve.* A coach who is lukewarm about winning a championship will get a lackluster team effort; a series of disjointed, selfish performances are likely. As a parent, you have to own a detailed vision of what your child will blossom into as an adult. Having that concept clear in your mind will enable you to develop a plan, with related benchmarks, that facilitates meaningful accountability and adjustments.

3. *Impact is derived by coaching "in the moment."* Your parenting efforts must take place in "real time," not days, hours, or even minutes after an event occurs. Even if your efforts seem redundant—"I've already told him about that"—an effective coach continually addresses the developmental needs of the child at the time when such feedback will have the greatest impact. People learn best from their experiences; providing insight as an experience unfolds is most helpful.

4. *Great coaches are great communicators.* Communication includes not only telling people what they need to know, but also observing pertinent behavior closely and listening carefully. Effective coaches—and parents—don't simply spew directions and critiques; they involve the young people they're coaching in a dialogue related to where they are heading, how they will get there, and how they could enhance the quality of their effort. The coach, like the parent, takes the lead in driving the

dialogue and must be lovingly candid. It is not a true democracy: The coach is in charge. However, based on the relationship that exists, both coach and student benefit from interactive exchanges that clarify what each party is thinking, instead of monologues that allow the coach to dominate rather than influence.

5. *The coach must have a comprehensive plan for reaching the "promised land."* Every parent knows that raising children requires flexibility. Child rearing is the art of handling the unexpected without losing sight of the ultimate goal. The countless surprises and challenges that arise cannot distract the coach from the goal: raising a God-honoring human being. A great coach stays focused on the information, skills, behaviors, and beliefs—the promised land—that the child should come to own. That means crafting a long-term schedule of what types of experiences, information, and skills might be introduced to assist in the child's development.

    As your children's primary coach in life and faith, you have a wonderful opportunity to add value to their lives, to society, and to the Kingdom of God. But coaching is an intentional and strategic venture. What's your game plan?

FAMILY CONDITIONS

As a researcher, I study data to identify relationships between different attributes. The studies The Barna Group and I conducted for this book produced several relationships that might be of interest to you as we consider the conditions under which successful parenting occurs. (Or they may just cause you anguish, depending upon where you are in your life cycle.) Consider the following.

Family size. We found that the fewer children a family has, the more likely they are to produce spiritual champions. Now, this is a statistical probability; it does not mean that large families are incapable of producing stellar servants of God, nor does it mean we did not encounter such families. It simply means that the chances of raising a spiritual champion increase if you have fewer children and decrease if you have more children.

Why is this true? It seems related to the distribution of resources. No matter how many children are in a family, the number of parents involved in the process is constant. Obviously, the more children you have, the less time and resources each of them can receive. Our findings suggest that the amount of time devoted to hands-on parenting is a significant factor; thus, having a large number of children may diminish the degree of parental attention focused on each one's spiritual development. Great parenting is indisputably labor intensive. It is certainly possible to raise healthy, decent kids in the midst of a large number of siblings, but raising a spiritual champion is facilitated by having greater access to parental resources than is likely in a larger family.

Birth order. Another insight gleaned from the research concerns birth order. The research showed that the firstborn is the child most likely to become a spiritual champion.

Whether this is because of the well-documented advantages of firstborn children (that is, undivided and heightened parental attention, as well as high expectations) or other factors is not clear. What is clear is that the oldest child is most likely to reap the benefits of being the first in the nest and to grow into a mature follower of Christ. (You may be nervously wondering: Is it possible to have a child who is not the firstborn become a spiritual champion? Absolutely; the research was pointing out probabilities, not certainties or absolute limitations.)

Family characteristics. Our research also noted that a family's socioeconomic status has no correlation with the spiritual development of a child. Household income level, parental educational achievement, age of the parents, ethnicity, and parental career path seem to have no relationship to the trajectory of a child's spiritual growth.

We did find a relationship between children's spirituality and the marital status of their parents. Single parents have a tougher time raising spiritual champions because the challenges that are normally distributed across two people's efforts must be facilitated by one person who may or may not be successful at introducing a team of outside helpers into the child-rearing mix. We found very few instances where a spiritual champion was the product of a single-family home. That does not mean it is impossible to raise a God-honoring child as a single parent, but the challenges are more substantial.[1]

Perhaps these insights lead us to a biblical principle: Before you have children, count the cost of raising them. The research suggests that the more children you have, the more difficult it will be to facilitate the spiritual health and depth of each child. That doesn't mean it cannot be done; it simply means you should be very aware of the challenges and be intentional in your choices.

PARENTING IS JOB ONE

A final condition for success that we discovered is that those who produce spiritual champions embrace parenting as their primary job in life. The nature of who their children will become assumes such importance that these parents recognize that their career is a means to the end of raising progeny who please God. Combined with the realization that effective parenting is conducted "in the moment," this means that parenting is their full-time job; the job they get paid to do is simply an addendum to the most important work they will do in life.

Again, the Bible encourages this perspective. In Deuteronomy, God tells His people the following:

You must love the LORD your God with all your heart, all your soul, and all your strength. And you must commit yourselves wholeheartedly to these commands that I am giving you today. Repeat them again and again to your children. Talk about them when you are at home and when you are on the road, when you are going to bed and when you are getting up. Tie them to your hands and wear them on your forehead as reminders. Write them on the doorposts of your house and on your gates.

(DEUTERONOMY 6:5-9)

After reiterating the nature of spiritual champions—people who love God with all of their hearts, minds, strength, and souls—God emphasizes that our job as parents is to live the biblical life and to spare no pains in keeping the matters of God first and foremost in the minds of our children. If the commands and principles of God are of such importance to Him, how can they be of any less significance to us?

From this passage we can see that God attaches great importance to how we instruct our children about life and faith. He clearly relies upon parents—not schools, churches, government, or friends—to raise children appropriately; it is our responsibility and one that He expects us to take seriously. And toward that end, He invites us to pull out all the stops in our attempts to create spiritual champions.

My interviews among Revolutionary Parents indicate that they accept and doggedly pursue this no-holds-barred approach. They are very intentional and focused on the heart and mind of each child in their homes. Such attentiveness does not by itself always produce the desired results, but anything less is almost guaranteed to produce failure.

Rapid Review

- You cannot control the outcome of your parenting efforts.
- Your responsibility is to be obedient to God in raising your children; you must leave the outcomes up to Him.
- Revolutionary Parents are great coaches.

- Count the costs involved in expanding your family.
- Socioeconomic factors do not provide an excuse for failing to produce spiritual champions.
- Parenting is your primary full-time job.

Hands-On

1. Think about the relationship you have with each of your children. Write down three things you will commit to do during the next thirty days that will improve your relationship with them.
2. Consider the lessons your children learn from watching you. Write down three things that you will change in your behavior during the next thirty days in order to have a more positive and biblical influence on the lives of your children.
3. Pray that God will give you the personal resources to make the changes you have written down—and that those transitions will enhance your ability to raise your children to be spiritual champions.

chapter three

REVOLUTIONARY PARENTS PUT FIRST THINGS FIRST

AMERICAN CULTURE DOES not support the notion of parenting being a full-time job. In fact, many in our society look down upon those individuals, most often women, who devote the largest share of their "business hours" energy to being stay-at-home parents. Such commitment is generally thought of as a luxury reserved for the affluent. The rest of the nation has to fit its parenting duties around the more pressing matters of earning a living (and maintaining a desirable lifestyle).

The dominant parenting philosophy of America is clear and widely accepted: Parents must do the best they can raising their kids on the fly and providing them with "quality time" and costly goodies meant to convey parental affection. At the same time, they must invest themselves wholeheartedly in "providing for the family" through career ascension, thus gaining the approval of fellow citizens who understand the challenge of the daily juggling act. In this context, American society enables and encourages parents to make child rearing a communal affair, relying upon institutions such as schools, community organizations, churches, the mass media, and government agencies to pick up the slack and cover for parents while they are trying to change the world in their nine-to-five roles.

PARENTING IS THE PRIMARY JOB

One of the important characteristics of Revolutionary Parents is that they remain unaffected by the cultural myths about parenting. Revolutionary Parents fight the cultural enticements and emotional temptation to embrace society's dominant parenting philosophy. They resist not because they are renegades or contrarian. They simply want to do what is right, based not on social norms but upon biblical principles.

Interestingly, we learned that although their countercultural approach to parenting places them squarely in a minority position, it causes Revolutionary Parents little stress or concern.

Nevertheless, this choice—and make no mistake about it, it is a choice, with all of the pros and cons associated with any choice we make—comes at a cost to the parents and their family.

One of the most significant effects is a radically realigned pool of personal and family relationships. Most Americans respect but do not relate to households in which parenting is taken so seriously. In fact, many parents view such an approach as a challenge or threat to their own family choices and ways of life. But parenting cannot be Revolutionary if it adopts the core assumptions and practices of the prevailing culture. Our research found that parents are more likely to raise spiritual champions if they accept the fact that from day one their parenting efforts will stray from the norm and will put them at odds with parents who are pursuing a more conventional approach.

Our study also revealed the following. Revolutionary Parents are more likely to:

- Be single-income households
- Schedule a much greater amount of time to spend with their children each day
- Intentionally identify their children as their main earthly focus in life during their parenting years

Making child rearing a top priority was just one of the qualities that differentiates the parents of spiritual champions. Let's examine some of the other quirks that enable them to produce notably different children.

GOD WINS FIRST PLACE

The willingness of Revolutionary Parents to make raising their children a paramount daily priority is based on their Christian faith as the pivot point of all their decisions. The parents we interviewed were unequivocal in their placement of their faith in Christ and their desire to be obedient to God as the guiding light of their life. (To be fair, many of them were quick to add that they are imperfect examples of basing every choice on biblical principles.)

From our research, we can posit that raising a spiritual champion is best accomplished by having at least one parent in the home who is fully committed to honoring God through his or her parenting practices.

Many of the parents in our research did not have an upbringing that prepared them to be spiritual champions, and many of them are not "superstar" Christians even today. However, having evaluated the options based on their life experiences, they had concluded that the greatest gift they could give their offspring was a sound upbringing based on biblical principles. That mind-set was a reflection of their personal campaign to integrate their faith in Christ into every dimension of their lives.

The ground-level reality, then, is that the decisions these parents make are tied back to biblical principles. They make choices based on their knowledge and interpretation of the Bible. The choices include how to discipline their youngsters; whether they require their kids to attend church services; whether they read and study the Bible as a family; and how they balance the importance of academics, social life, and faith. The parents we studied made different choices because of their distinctive biblical interpretations—but they all defended their decisions based on their understanding of biblical perspectives.

GROWING SPIRITUALLY, TOGETHER

One of the idiosyncrasies of these families is that they tend to delve into faith matters as a family unit. While there are ample instances of family members engaging in spiritual activities apart from other family members—for example, Sunday school classes, small-group involvement, attending Christian events—the glue that holds it all together consists of two themes:

- family conversations that bring biblical views into their shared lives, and
- efforts to regularly engage in faith activities (Bible study, worship, prayer) that model the integration of faith into their lives.

This practice is certainly an aberration, even among families in which one or both parents are born-again Christians. Nationwide, fewer than one out of every ten born-again families read the Bible together during a typical week or pray together during a typical week, excluding mealtimes. Discussing faith principles as a normal part of decision making is highly unusual, even in "Christian" America.

But many of the Revolutionary Parents we interviewed underscored how crucial these family faith experiences were to raising a godly child.

"If they [her children] did not get the experience of thinking about and talking about their faith at home, they would not have had the experience," stated one of the mothers who raised a spiritual champion. "When I grew up, we never talked about spiritual matters. So when I went to school or work,

I was intimidated by the subject. My husband and I made sure that would not be the case with our children. So we prayed out loud with them, all the time. We read the Bible together, and when we disciplined the kids, we'd often go and look up a verse to show them that our choices were not random or weird, but just following the heart of the Lord. And all of that openness about our faith made them more comfortable discussing their faith and even thinking about how to make their faith a central part of who they are and how they live. I'm so proud of them for that commitment and the way they live their faith today."

The adult children we interviewed realized that their parents were different when it came to faith and that their religious expectations for them were quite unlike those experienced by their friends. However, three out of every four of those children said they rarely, if ever, resented the pervasive spiritual influence and the substantial religious activity expected of them. A similar three-quarters of the parents expressed the belief that such direct involvement in the spiritual life of their kids, and holding them to high standards of participation, was crucial to their spiritual development. In fact, the adult children stated that it was the extensive time spent studying the Bible as a family that made the greatest difference in their emergence as dedicated followers of Christ and advocates of Scripture.

A GENUINE RELATIONSHIP

Television shows and movies frequently parody the absence of a genuine relationship between children and their parents.

With good reason, media often depict the parent-child relationship as one based upon occasionally overlapping mealtimes or sharing space in the living room while watching a TV program of mutual interest (if one can be found!).

One of the moving aspects of our research was discovering the depth of love that Revolutionary Parents had for their children and how that translated into an intense sense of mission to prepare them for life. These parents held the notion that ministry is relational in nature and their ability to affect the lives of their children would be minimized unless their love for their children was manifested in an authentic relationship. That did not limit their willingness to institute parameters, maintain significant standards of character and performance, and enforce discipline. It simply meant that they were striving to fulfill a dual role: that of real friend and that of authoritative coach.

Revolutionary Parents recognize that children have basic physical and psychological needs, such as security, safety, significance, affirmation, acceptance, and love, that must be met. But the way they deliver those elements to their children is often through the conduit of a relationship built on trust and constant interaction. Conversations about moral and spiritual matters occur more frequently and easily because of that connection.

The research revealed an amazing insight into just how much time was spent in dialogue between parent and child on a typical day. The figures ranged between 90 and 120 minutes (verified by both the parent and child, independent of each other). To place that in context, the typical American family registers less than fifteen minutes of direct parent-child conversation each day. Imagine what a difference it would make if you had six times as much daily verbal interaction with your child!

SPIRITUAL GROWTH IS INTENTIONAL

What fosters Revolutionary Parents' ability to consistently honor God through parenting and provide their children with a stellar upbringing? According to our research, they intentionally pursue faith maturity. The Revolutionary Parents interviewed did not hesitate to explain the personal significance of seeking their own spiritual growth on a daily basis. They worked at it and enjoyed it, and it made a discernible difference in what they had to offer their children.

Our interviews with the adult children who had been raised by these parents confirmed that the consistent effort and emphasis placed on spiritual growth made an impression on their young minds. Although most of them admitted that at the time they did not understand the implications, they now said that the commitment to growth seen in their parents' life was largely responsible for the depth of character and faith their parents drew from at the time. Those adult children also noted that the example set by their parents continues to have an effect on how these young adults live today.

Rapid Review

- Focusing upon raising spiritual champions was the chief obligation in life of the Revolutionary Parents we interviewed.

- Faith in God is very real and central in the lives of Revolutionary Parents. That faith is perceived as the most valuable asset they can transfer to their children.
- Raising a champion for Christ requires developing and sustaining an authentic relationship with the child, based on love and trust.
- The Christian faith of Revolutionary Parents must be continually maturing.

Hands-On

1. Examine your real priorities in life—not those to which you give lip service, but those demonstrated by your calendar, your checkbook, and your emotions. What stands in the way of making your children a top priority in your life?
2. How comfortable is your family spending time together, several times a week, exploring God's Word, sharing openly during prayer sessions, and engaging in conversations that relate your faith principles to your critical life choices? What could you introduce into your family's dynamics to make faith a more natural centerpiece of such discussions and activities?
3. If your children were asked to honestly assess your personal commitment to growing deeper in your faith, what kind of rating would they give? How satisfied are you with your personal investment in growing spiritually? What might you do to foster a more fulfilling spiritual journey?

chapter four

REVOLUTIONARY PLANNING FOR SPIRITUAL CHAMPIONS

ACROSS AMERICA, ADULTS generally hold the belief that our nation's children are inadequately prepared morally or spiritually for their future. In fact, more than three out of every five parents believe that the younger generation is not ready to handle an increasingly complex and demanding future.

One of the reasons why our youngsters are so vulnerable is that few adults have clearly and comprehensively thought through their role as parents. I have conducted research studies involving more than a half million people over the past quarter century. During that period I have observed some consistent elements about human decision making and behavior. One of those insights is that few people have a well-defined philosophy that guides their every move.

This seems to be especially true when it comes to parenting. Most of the parents we've interviewed in recent years have a survival-based philosophy rather than a goal-oriented philosophy.

While one must be careful not to accept people's retrospective explanations for their behavior as a perfect reflection of past reality, our interviews with the parents of spiritually transformed children showed that they had a refreshingly unambiguous notion of their role. Here is a description of some of the key perspectives that influenced their parenting efforts.

GET IN THE GAME EARLY

Most parents—especially first-timers—juggle the desire to enjoy their child's early years with meeting their non-stop needs amidst sleepless nights. That makes putting into practice the first gem of wisdom from Revolutionary Parents sound impossible. But it is crucial.

Here it is: Start your Revolutionary Parenting while your children are very young, and be relentlessly diligent from that point on.

Whether Revolutionary Parents we studied made that choice on the basis of instinct or information, this advice is sound. Many studies confirm that children begin absorbing values and beliefs as soon as they can understand language. Conventional wisdom reminds us that children are sponges, absorbing everything in their environment, whether we want them to or not. Think of all the opportunities they have to pick up life perspectives: television content (both audio and visual cues), music (from the car radio to sound tracks of movies and TV shows), dinner-table and household conversations they hear, and so on.

Great parents recognize that from the moment a child leaves the womb until the time he or she leaves the home, they must tirelessly guard and shape the mind, heart, and soul of their child.

Looking back on their experience, more than a few of the outstanding parents we spoke to admitted that there were times when they simply let down their guard out of fatigue, confusion, frustration, or ignorance. These parents uniformly noted that such lapses in attention can produce undesirable outcomes in their children, even if those lapses simply open the door to future difficulties.

Some parents noted the importance of the mother and father working together well to give each other a break, to look out for things the other did not see, and to provide the child with comprehensive care. The tag-team approach is a particularly useful tactic when there are multiple children requiring parental attention.

PLAN IT, MEASURE IT, REVISE IT

Another of the distinctive qualities of Revolutionary Parents was that they set tangible and measurable parenting goals and held themselves accountable. (Chapter 8 focuses on the types of goals they set.) Three out of every four of these parents (73 percent) developed and pursued goals. That's about fifteen times the proportion among other parents.

"I had to learn the hard way," explained one of the effective parents, "that unless I sat down, thought through where we were going as parent and child, how I was going to get there, and then developed some steps or milestones along the way that would show me whether or not I was making progress, my efforts quickly deteriorated into satisfaction with getting through the day without doing anyone bodily harm. Having a plan and some benchmarks was really important for me."

Every parent knows that even the best-developed plans are hard to execute. Inevitably, life's unknown and unexpected events and influences muscle their way into your experience and wreak havoc with those carefully conceived plans. But the potential for failure is no excuse not to prepare for success. Every respectable military strategist, educator, business manager, political leader, and effective parent will agree that achieving positive outcomes rarely happens by chance. It is almost always the result of good planning and diligent implementation.

Equally critical is assessment along the way. By that I mean evaluating each day what went right, what went wrong, and how you can improve your parenting efforts tomorrow based on what you learned today. Maybe another way of describing this dimension of Revolutionary Parenting is that you learn from your experiences every day and adjust your efforts based on the desired goals and the new information gathered.

In practical terms, this requires that parents have a clear list of values and objectives that define acceptable outcomes. Matching a child's words and behaviors against that list gives parents something tangible to use in helping their children develop appropriate habits. Of course, this process can become unwieldy if the list of targeted outcomes is too detailed. Revolutionary Parents seem skilled at identifying the dimensions of life that make a significant difference and then focusing on those elements. Over time, if a child seems to have mastered a particular value, it might be replaced on the list with a different behavior that advances his or her maturation.

FORGET THE ONE-SIZE-FITS-ALL APPROACH

In egalitarian America, the idea of treating each child differently is not highly regarded. Most of the parents we have interviewed in the general population acknowledged that their kids are different, but believe that their parenting behavior toward each child must be nearly identical to be fair.

Revolutionary Parents don't buy that line of reasoning. They have operated on the principle—very successfully—that because each of their youngsters is unique, their parenting responses must be unique as well. Yes, there are a few golden principles that they adhere to in disciplining and educating each child. For instance, they may believe that showing compassion to their children is necessary, but what constitutes compassion for one child (such as allowing a normally diligent child to miss school for a minor ailment) might be detrimental to another child (reinforcing a lackadaisical child's manipulative tendency).

One reason for the differentiation is the recognition that God has wired every person differently. Each of us has a unique blend of personality types, spiritual gifts, natural talents, dreams, and limitations that can be maximized if we understand that mixture and try to draw out the strengths and not worry about areas that are not strong. Ninety-six percent of the Revolutionary Parents we interviewed took the time and made the effort to learn the unique nature of each of their children and to build a parenting framework around each child's distinctives.

Listen, can you hear it? That's the sound of siblings yelling about the favoritism shown to others in the family by the parents. Despite the wisdom embedded in treating each child in a unique way for their own good, great parents will always encounter opposition from the children who feel that they are getting a raw deal. Even though the children in question grew up to become spiritual champions, they threw their hissy fits over alleged improper practices engaged in by their parents. To their credit, this did not deter the parents from pursuing what they believed was the best course of action.

"Children see things from a different perspective than a parent does," explained one parent. "But that's why God put us in charge and did not leave them to fend for themselves. I have to know my child and love him enough to do what's best, whether he likes it or not. Each child is a different person, so it would not make sense for me to treat each one the same. My husband and I gave them the same love and attention and care, but we tried to fit our approach to the different personality and capacity of each child."

A one-size-fits-all approach to parenting is easier, but it certainly does not produce better results. To take a simple example, consider a boy whose gifts and abilities lie in the creative field and his sister who yearns for the clarity of parameters and the application of well-defined structure. These children—raised in the same home by the same parents—benefit from different forms of discipline, different types of experiences, and divergent types of discussions with the parents about how they interpret and respond to life. The girl who gains security and discernment from fitting within clear structure and understanding of the rules is likely to flounder if those boundaries are removed or not consistently enforced. But her brother, who naturally thinks outside the box, would feel stifled by the imposition of too much claustrophobic structure.

In Revolutionary Parenting, the children know there are basic values and expectations that will be enforced at all times—honesty, cleanliness, thrift, concern for others, and so forth. But individuals are given the freedom to express themselves in personalized ways that are consistent with those values.

Perhaps not surprisingly, finding the right blend of freedom and limitations proved to be a taxing proposition for the parents we interviewed.

"It was a lot of trial and error for us until we found the right combination for each of our children," reported a father of three boys, who have ventured in different directions vocationally. "My wife and I sensed early on that we had three very different people on our hands, and that we would have to tailor our parenting to take account of those differences. Boy, did we make a lot of mistakes along the way, because it's sometimes really hard to read the situation right. But kids are pretty resilient, and if they feel assured that you love them and that you are trying to do what is best for them, they give you enough grace to get through the process. But there were many sleepless nights as my wife and I tried to figure out what certain responses from the boys meant and what our next move would be. It was kind of like an unending chess game where you want everyone to win."

DON'T PUSH IT

Living in a culture that esteems achievement and speed, parents naturally want to hurry the development of their offspring. We discovered, however, that one of the core philosophies of Revolutionary Parents was to advance their children at a pace that was natural for the child. They held on to this position even when teachers, family members, or friends expressed disapproval.

"You can't worry too much about how other people judge your decisions," cautioned one parent. "They are not responsible and they are not living with the child. They can do what they want with their kids; I have to live with the consequences of my choices for my children. That always helped me to shut out the criticisms of others. I tried to stay focused on the needs of my children, not the reactions of outsiders."

In our studies of what takes place in school classrooms and even Sunday school classes around the nation, we often have encountered the alarming trend of identifying what children "should" be like at a given age, along with the institutional push to make sure they reach that stage at the appointed time. In countless cases it has seemed as if children's development is being rushed to satisfy some ambiguous goal, robbing them of the delights of childhood in an effort to usher them into the responsibilities of adulthood prematurely. We hurry to get them there, then wonder why they seem discontent or unfulfilled. Sometimes we inadvertently "fast-track" personal development, eliminating the joy of growing at the pace God ordained for the person.

We've all heard of late bloomers and prodigies, although we seem to have less exposure to such concepts these days. It takes a special form of parenting—one filled with patience, understanding, clear purpose, and gentleness—to allow a child to mature less quickly than his or her peers, simply because it seems right for that child. It also takes a special parent to foster the prodigious talents and interests of the truly gifted or even a genuine prodigy (not a child who is simply pushed to outperform classmates in areas the parent esteems).

"My parents pushed me when I was young," recalled the father of two children. "At the time I did not know any better, and I went along with it. But looking back, I feel sad that I missed out on so much of what I would have liked to have experienced, or even that I couldn't have just taken it a bit slower. What's the hurry? They'll be adults soon enough, and they'll be adults for the rest of their lives. I resolved to let my kids enjoy every possible moment of being a child. . . . I knew I wouldn't be doing them any favors by pushing them to arrive before their friends, or before they're ready. God's timing for my children was perfect. It was my job to figure out that timing and orchestrate it as best I could. My wife and I took a bunch of grief from others, especially my in-laws, but we had to do what we felt was best for the kids. Looking at them today, I think we did the right thing."

Again, this approach means allowing each child to emerge in a way that reflects who God made him or her to be. Just as each of us has unique fingerprints, so God has crafted each of us with a different mix of qualities and capabilities, which need to be nurtured in a reasonable manner. If we look for the teaching moments that enable our children to grasp a concept or principle, and seize those moments so that we can build on them in a progressive developmental experience, we need not rely upon a forced model of rapid development. Allowing your child to get pleasure from growing at his or her God-ordained pace is a blessing.

FOCUS ON CHARACTER

In a quarter century of doing research I have rarely encountered instances where 100 percent of the group being studied agreed on something. Yet every single Revolutionary Parent we interviewed agreed that the most important focus of their children's training was the development of godly character.

This may sound like a no-brainer. However, if you examine the outcomes we strive to achieve in our households, our schools, and our youth programs such as sports, you will discover that there are two dominant outcomes sought: honing skills and grasping information. Little emphasis is placed upon overt character development. In speaking with the adults in charge of these spheres of influence, it became clear that the assumption is that if a child learns the information and skills being imparted, good character will naturally emerge.

That is one of the great lies of the age.

What are some of the critical character traits we should look for in a child's development?

Honesty	Compassion	Love
Kindness	Patience	Joy
Gentleness	Self-control	Loyalty
Reliability	Consistency	Perseverance
Encouragement	Humility	Justice
Mercy	Maturity	Stability
Discipline	Trustworthiness	Sincerity

Spiritual champions have the advantage of being raised by parents who are more concerned about the love they show fellow students than whether they outperform them. They are raised to tell the truth, even if it means they might lose some opportunities. They are leaders in the Christian community as adults because their example speaks for itself—an example based upon a solid character that was guided by parents who believed that character does not magically emerge without intentional effort and that who you are matters a lot more than what you accomplish.

The great parents we interviewed remember that it was much easier teaching the alphabet or multiplication than shaping the character of their child, but they forged ahead anyway.

"Oh my gosh," said a mother, laughing as she recalled the behavior of her son, who was always trying to impress his folks with his grades and his sports feats. "We kept coming back to how he treated people and what he did with his money and what kind of stories he'd tell his friends. We tried to affirm his accomplishments, but we worked at keeping those things in their proper place. He was sick of hearing me tell him that I'd rather have an honest boy than a smart one, and that God was more excited about a servant than a superstar. It took him a long time to get that message. None of his friends were being given the message, his teachers did not give him that message, his coaches did not give him that message; it was only dorky Mom and Dad who kept harping on that theme. But as he grew older and began to see, and sometimes suffer from, the absence of character among his friends, he latched onto the idea that character matters more than achievements."

ROLL UP YOUR SLEEVES

Parents, by definition, are busy people. They not only orchestrate the corporate activities of the family, they have personal lives that include a vocation, friendships, health care, leisure pursuits, spiritual growth, and more. They have direct input into the individual lives of their children. They are generally active in a variety of community endeavors, ranging from sports leagues to church. The bottom line is simple: Parents must use their time judiciously.

That may mean different things to different parents,

though. While we found that most parents in the United States limit the areas of life in which they are intimately involved with their children, Revolutionary Parents tend to be much more hands-on, in-the-trenches active. More than eight out of every ten of them said they were heavily involved in every aspect of their child's life.

Perhaps one way of defining the difference between typical parents and Revolutionary Parents, then, is to identify the most challenging balance each is attempting to master.

Most parents try to balance their personal needs and those of their children, seeking to limit their input in the relationships and decisions of their children as much as possible. Their view is that providing general guidelines and allowing children to learn through trial and error is the best course of action. The challenge, in other words, is to know when they need to devote more time and energy to their children.

Revolutionary Parents, on the other hand, attempt to subjugate their own breadth of needs in order to be a partner with the child in every dimension of his or her life. The balance they most often struggle with is where to draw the line between helpful assistance and overbearing intruder. It is taken for granted that they will devote dozens of hours each week to interacting with their children; the challenge for them is to know how much is too much.

The distinction between the two categories of parents, then, is the difference between knowing when to ramp it up and when to back off.

"Kids get in trouble when they do not have enough

supervision or guidance," remarked one parent, summarizing the perspective embraced by many Revolutionary Parents. "Our job as parents is to be there, right next to them, to help them learn how to identify the issues and how to make proper choices. We have to be involved enough to help them know how to follow through on their choices and to reinforce the good choices they have embraced. Too many parents stay at arm's length, assuming their kids will know what to do and will approach them if they encounter problems. But a lot of times their kids don't even know what a problem is, or they do not feel comfortable bringing it up with the parent. It is that kind of hands-off parenting that invites problems to occur."

The solution, to Revolutionary Parents, is to translate the notion of parenting as their highest calling into investing substantial amounts of time and energy into their relationship with the child and the activities in which he or she engages.

"When I thought through my schedule each morning," recalled one active mother, "I always tried to anticipate when my boys would need my attention and simply cleared out everything to allow for that. If it turned out that they did not need me for the entire block of time, then I had some free time that I could use to finish my other tasks, but their needs were always at the top of my priority list. My job was to be their mother, not simply a cohabitant in our house. My husband held the same view. When he got home from work, tired as he was, he knew his first priority was to make sure he was involved in their lives, from schoolwork and sports to spiritual nurturing and moral development. It's both exhausting and fulfilling, but for us it was pretty much all-consuming."

The greatest tension these parents experienced was related to becoming too involved—smothering their child through well-intended but excessive participation. But these parents regularly tinkered with their levels of engagement, seeking the best balance so that their children might welcome the input of their parents while maturing through their own experimentation.

MAKE FRIENDS ELSEWHERE

Parenting, it turns out, is not a popularity contest. While many parents approach this adventure as one in which they are trying to win the emotional approval of their youngsters, parents who raised spiritual champions generally rejected that approach. They wanted their children to love and appreciate them, of course, but many of these parents echoed the idea that they were not trying to become the child's best friend.

"My personal security was found in Christ. My best friend is my wife. My son was my gift to God, to the church, and to the world," was the perspective of a father of a young man who is a leader in his local Christian community. "If I was determined to win over my boy as my best friend, I would have pandered in ways that are inappropriate for someone responsible for his growth as a man of God. We had many a tense moment over the years, but I don't think there was ever any doubt in his mind that I loved him, or about the motivation behind the hard choices and discipline I enforced in his life. And naturally I wanted him to be proud of me, to like spending time with me, and to share his life with me. But part of being a good parent is making the choice to be a parent, not a best friend. Hopefully, by doing your job as a parent lovingly and effectively, the child recognizes what you're doing and why, and accepts your efforts for the value they bring into their life."

Our national research has shown that most parents are quite concerned about others' perception of them. In fact, many determine how they will parent based on how they think their actions will be evaluated by their friends and extended family. However, that viewpoint conflicts with the mind-set of Revolutionary Parents.

"I heard about the names that other parents called me," said a Revolutionary mother, now in her sixties. "But I couldn't worry about that. It hurt me, of course. There were times I cried to myself because of the mean, nasty things that people would say about our family and about me, in particular. But I kept reminding myself that I didn't raise my children for the approval of the world, but for the glory of God. If I could feel good about the things I did because I felt they honored Him and that I'd prepared my children to love and serve God, then the sting of the gossip was decreased. Maybe it boils down to who you're trying to please: God, the children, or your neighbors."

Interestingly, our research among young adults revealed that most of them believed that parents are often too lenient with their children.

"When I was growing up, I never would have said this,"

said one young Revolutionary Christian, laughing. "But now, as I look at the lives of my childhood friends, the ones I envied because they had so much freedom when we were growing up, their lives are a mess. I'm not perfect, but I think I understand life a lot better and have a better foundation for life. Now I have all the appreciation in the world for the tough stands my parents took to keep me in check. Kids can't handle too much freedom; they're children! I thank God regularly that my parents put up with all the whining and complaining from me and my brothers and sisters but did not give in. They held their ground, and I think the results of their efforts are a real blessing to God and the community."

PARENT-PROVIDED STRUCTURE

Childhood is an unnerving period. You're physically small and limited. You lack the financial resources to get things done. You're bombarded with a host of spiritual perspectives, many of which seem amorphous and unrealistic. Friends come and go. The family might move, requiring you to start over in terms of relationships and routines. Siblings have their own agendas. School is competitive but not terribly rewarding. News outlets focus on bad news—enough to make you jittery about the state of the world.

In short, there's not much about the daily experience of children that delivers stability, security, and reliability.

Great parents stand in the gap to provide their children with the structure and solidarity that make the ambiguities of daily life less onerous. They do this by establishing and consistently enforcing rules. They assign roles and household functions to everyone in the family. They clarify their relationship and corresponding duties connected to citizenship, church membership, their community, extended family, marriage, and team membership.

One of the most intriguing comments in our research was made by a young woman raised by Revolutionary Parents. Now the mother of two preschoolers, she pointed out one of the great treasures her parents had given her.

"Most of the kids I grew up with did not have a stable family life. I think a majority of them had parents who had been or were in the process of getting divorced. I spent a lot of time thinking about that. All the girls would talk, in intimate moments we shared, about what they felt while their parents were raging at each other, or when their parents split up—it was awful. They felt scared; they felt like it must have been their fault; they felt trapped in an ugly environment. It gave me reason to think about the fact that my parents regularly told us and showed us that they were not going to break up, that they'd be there over the long haul for me and my brothers. That made me feel pretty secure and strong, like I at least had a place and a family that I could count on to be there for me. I had other issues that frightened me, but the strength that came from knowing Mom and Dad would always be there, waiting for me, caring for me, was a pretty big deal. That gave me self-confidence and minimized my anxieties about life."

One factor that repeatedly drew attention among the

children who became spiritual champions was the dependability they had in their home environment. The consistency of people, roles, and choices seemed to provide these young people with a series of lifestyle variables they could eliminate as possible anxiety factors.

How was that stability and continuity manifested? We heard the following:

- Revolutionary Parents verbalized the conditions that would remain stable: marriage, household rules, moral expectations, financial priorities, and so on.
- Revolutionary Parents carried out their promises: What they said would remain in effect did, indeed, remain in effect.
- Revolutionary Parents expected children to maintain consistency in their behavior, following through on the rules and roles that were in place.
- Revolutionary Parents espoused a philosophy of life or worldview and beliefs that provided a level of predictability children found to be soothing.

"At school, the teachers were inconsistent in how they reinforced their rules. At church, everyone was too nice to enforce much of anything. But at home," reflected a grown child of Revolutionary Parents, "I could always count on what my parents said being carried out, or their expectations of me and my brothers and sisters being fairly enforced. As aggravating as that was sometimes—you couldn't get away with anything—it was also a relief to know that there was some order to the universe, even if it was only on our property. That was kind of encouraging to me when I was young; I could count on Mom and Dad to do what they said, or to hold us accountable for their expectations."

LET THE CHURCH HELP—NOT LEAD

Parents who raised spiritual champions certainly placed a high premium on the spiritual development of their children. But the fascinating distinctive is that they saw themselves as the primary spiritual developers of their young ones. The role of the church to which they belonged—whether it was a conventional congregation, a house church, or some other alternative community of faith—was to reinforce what was happening in the household.

"I never expected, or wanted, my pastor or even my church to be responsible for the spiritual condition of my children," noted one mother. "I bore those children, and God called me and my husband to take full responsibility for their growth. If I went to a doctor, I'd weigh his advice and only follow it if it made sense. If a teacher had some criticism of my child, I'd accept it only if it seemed reasonable. It's no different with our faith. The local church was very important for our family and in the raising of our children, but not as the place that was responsible for their spiritual growth. That responsibility was given to me and my husband by God, so we just leaned on the church for help, not leadership."

One of the fascinating differences between the views of Revolutionary Parents and typical parents is their reaction to the youth leaders of their church. Revolutionary Parents want to know what those individuals teach, what they expect of their students, how they conduct the experience, and how they want to interact with the parents. If the youth leader does not satisfy their standards, these parents are likely to yank their children from the group, or at least to eliminate pressure on their children to regularly participate in those group meetings.

In contrast, typical parents know little about the content and conduct of their church's ministry to young people beyond details related to time and place. They rarely consider withdrawing their children from the program because the mere presence of their children in the class is an end in itself.

Sadly, our studies confirm that most Protestant churches consider ministry to children to be a very low priority: Only 15 percent of the senior pastors of Protestant churches identify this ministry as one of the top priorities of their church. The average budget further exhibits the low value assigned by church leaders to children's ministry: People under the age of thirteen represent about two-fifths of the bodies that set foot on church campuses, but they are awarded less than one-seventh of the dollars spent by those congregations.[1]

We found a correlation between parental expectations of their church's children's ministry and their satisfaction with it. The more specific and the higher their substantive expectations for the ministry, the less satisfied parents were. Conversely, parents who were generally satisfied just to have access to a children's ministry with adult supervision and resources accessible by the group were more likely to be satisfied by the ministry. Not surprisingly, Revolutionary Parents were more likely to be among the former group.

SEE THE HORIZON

One thing that American parents agree upon, whether they raise spiritual champions or not: It is easy to get discouraged in the process of raising children! One way Revolutionary Parents handle the challenging role is by remaining aware that the ultimate results of their child-rearing efforts will not be known for years. Raising kids in today's world is a war; losing one battle in the war does not constitute losing the war itself.

This, of course, relates to the perspective of Revolutionary Parents: They take the long-term view, not the in-the-moment view that can cause emotional paralysis if taken out of context. Great parents know that every day has the potential to generate a step backward in their child's life—morally, spiritually, intellectually, physically, or relationally. But as is true in life overall, sometimes it takes a bit of failure to produce a load of success. Seeing things in the appropriate context can make all the difference between giving up and digging deeper.

Revolutionary Parents have the advantage of believing that they are raising their children in tandem with God. They do not see themselves as raising their young ones in a vacuum. Their confidence in God's desire and ability to support them, as well as their belief that God cares deeply about the well-being and maturity of their children, helps them remain hopeful in the face of adversity. Interacting at their church or in other settings with young adults who have emerged as spiritual champions reminds them that it is possible to raise such children. Their perspective on God and their connection to living examples of the grace of God in people's lives enable them to recognize setbacks—and even victories—as momentary shifts in momentum that have to be interpreted within the larger context of the child's journey. And theirs.

Rapid Review

- The world begins influencing the values and beliefs of your children sooner than you may think. You've got to join the fray when your children are very young.
- Set reasonable goals for your children and stick with them.
- Every child requires a unique strategy and plan. You can apply the same principles with each child, but you must customize the implementation.
- Don't force your little people to become big people before they're ready. Let them develop at a pace that suits their God-given makeup.
- Nothing will serve your children better than working on instilling godly character.
- Use your time well; establish your parenting priorities and major on them.

- You're not out to be your child's best friend, only his or her best parent.
- Your kids need stability; provide the structure that gives the support they need.
- Use your local church as a support system, not as the leader of your children's spiritual development journey.
- Never lose sight of the big picture of what you are striving to facilitate. Daily nuisances can get to you if you're not careful.

Hands-On

1. You will get tired, distracted, and frustrated. What steps can you take to be sure that when you get weak, you don't let down your guard and enable your children to suffer the consequences?
2. You and your spouse must be an effective parenting team. What would improve your teamwork? If you are a single parent, who constitutes your team, and what steps can you take to improve the joint impact you have?
3. Teachers and coaches rarely recognize the unique needs of each child. What can you do to alert them to the developmental pace and nuances of your child?
4. Make a list of the character traits described in the Bible. What exercises and applications will enable you to help your child embody those characteristics?

5. Get to know the leaders of your children's ministry. Let them know the types of things you're doing and working on at home. That may help them to be a better support to you.

chapter five

THE RULES OF REVOLUTIONARY ENGAGEMENT

BATTLE STRATEGISTS HISTORICALLY have made great gains in war by pushing their enemy to fight simultaneously on multiple fronts. Forcing a foe to stretch resources thin and make other difficult choices can allow the aggressor to exploit the opponent's weaknesses. The side that misjudges the challenges is the one most vulnerable to attack—and defeat.

Parenting might be understood in that same light. The lives of children are so complex these days—with countless activities, connections, expectations, and the like—that parents have to pick their battles carefully. No parent is capable of fighting every battle that emerges in the war to train and protect their children. Great parenting is the art of providing sufficient education and experience so that children are willing and capable of making appropriate choices without having to go toe-to-toe with their parents on every issue, under all circumstances.

Although in our research we encountered a significant percentage of parents across the nation who said a good parent must fight every battle, we found that Revolutionary Parents disagreed.[1] Overall, 96 percent of them said you would wear yourself out and lose your relationship with your child if you fought them over every circumstance on which you disagreed. Those who have raised spiritual champions see their parenting as establishing the certainty of their love for their children, knowing what wisdom to impart, sharing significant experiences to train them for the future, providing pointed feedback regarding the choices they make, and backing off the rest of the time to allow the children to grow through personal experience.

Great parents admit that some battles are not only worth fighting, they *must* be strategically waged if the best interests of the child are to be served. How do you figure out which battles are in the "must" category? Here is a description of the challenges that Revolutionary Parents have found to be worth undertaking.

LAY DOWN THE LAW

One of the time-honored paradoxes of raising children is that young people chafe under the rules imposed by their parents—until they are mature enough to recognize the value those boundaries have incorporated into their character. The parent who thinks he is doing his child a favor by cutting the youngster slack will likely discover that providing such freedom does not serve the child well. The tension we feel over how much leeway to give is nothing new. As far back as the Garden of Eden, people have questioned the viability of rules.

You know, even without the benefit of confirmation from our research, that the combinations of rules that parents assign to their children are virtually incalculable. Yet, when asking Revolutionary Parents to identify the chief rules they relied upon with their children, we found a dozen or so common threads that might serve as a valuable foundation to consider.

Those widespread rules included the following.

- Always tell the truth, regardless of the circumstances or consequences; strive to be known as honest, reliable, and trustworthy.
- Never cheat or steal; that brings dishonor on yourself and disrespect to the victim.
- Always show respect to other people, no matter how you feel about them, through your attitude and language; it reflects the love that God has for them.
- Help others whenever the opportunity arises; we are servants.
- Control your tongue: Swearing and angry words are inappropriate.
- Do not judge other people's motives; only judge their behavior insofar as it personally affects you or family members.
- Take good care of your body; consistent hygiene and physical exercise are important to maintain.
- Be active in the pursuit of your faith, in whatever form that journey takes.

- Work hard in school to produce the best grades and most excellent work possible.
- Carry out your household chores as a means of pulling your weight in the family, honoring family members through service, and developing good habits.
- Make sure at least one parent knows where you are at all times; if you're away from home and want to go somewhere else, get parental approval first.
- Accept the penalties for inappropriate behavior; it is not a sign of anger or dislike by the elders who discipline you but a sign of caring and love designed to facilitate growth.

The critical ingredients to garnering successful outcomes from the application of these rules were that the child knew and understood them; that they were consistently enforced; that they were enforced without malice; and that both parents operated in agreement and with consistency.

Our research revealed that the spiritual champions we looked at grew up to appreciate the discipline provided by their parents through such rules. In fact, when we asked them what they believe is the most common mistake of American parents, the top answer was this: failing to identify and enforce a schedule of rules. Some of these same individuals admitted that when they were young they ranted about the injustice of the regulations and vowed they would never impose such a burden on their own children. They realize today how foolish such statements were and said they intend to carry on the tradition of laying down the law—and enforcing it—when they have their own children.

ENFORCE A CURFEW

You don't hear much about curfews anymore. We live in a 24-7 society, where the Internet is always available, stores are open round the clock, hundreds of television channels and radio stations battle for an audience at all hours of the day, and people are guilty of getting too little sleep as they strive to maximize their consumption of the pleasures of life.

Nevertheless, Revolutionary Parents affirm the importance of placing time limits on children.

"They'll stay up all night if you let them," acknowledged one parent. "During the summer, when they were teenagers, we relaxed their bedtime but often found that they fell asleep in the middle of whatever task they were pushing themselves to do. They'd wake up groggy the next day, but they kept pushing themselves to stay up late. We had to always hustle them into bed and monitor whether the lights and music were kept off. They were sneaky little devils when it came to trying to get in another hour or two at night."

Another facet of curfews relates to the time at which the children must be home. The time shifted as the child aged, but few of the Revolutionary Parents allowed curfews later than 11 p.m. on Fridays and Saturdays, even during summer vacation.

"There'd be exceptions, with school dances or travel to special events such as concerts or ball games," explained one father, "but those were certainly the exception to the rule. The rule was, in the house by nine or ten, lights out by ten or eleven, depending on the child and the circumstances. We learned early on that we could not make too many exceptions, because once they learned exceptions were possible, everything became a sufficient reason, in their mind, to qualify for an extension."

One of the ancillary expectations for most of these families was that if their child was outside the home after dark, another child's parent had to be present, and the parents had to know the company their child was keeping.

"We were adamant about knowing the facts: Where are you? Who are you with? What parent is accessible and responsible? What is the activity? When will you be home?" recalled the mother of one of the most popular kids in her school. "If we were lied to, or our needs were not met by their choices while out and about, there'd be a price to pay. They knew, and they treaded carefully."

The most common response to curfew abuse by children was being "grounded." That commonly would mean not being allowed to leave home except for school or family endeavors such as church. Such penalties tended to be rather stiff by typical standards: Lateness or other miscues resulted in having their privileges removed for a week or more, depending on the infraction.

"They knew there was no leeway; play by the rules or pay the price. We had some intense discussions the first time or two, but when they saw that we were serious and were willing to enforce the penalty, they complied very well. They always test you. You have to be ready to back up your words with action, or they'll trample you."

Things have changed in the past decade with the advent of cell phones in the hands of millions of children. Telecom firms have promoted "family phone plans" as one way to expand their market and hook a younger generation on the technology. Despite the widespread acceptance of mobile phones, some of the Revolutionary Parents interviewed remain cautious about relying too much on cell phones to keep the child in touch and safe.

"There's still a principle involved regarding responsibility and visibility," one parent cautioned. "It's too easy for young children to make a call and insist that everything's under control. A parent always has to have their antennae up for a scam. If kids figure a phone call buys them more freedom, the potential for trouble is increased. You have to trust your kids to a certain extent, but you also have to realize that they're always pushing the limits. Technology can be helpful, but it's no substitute for having a hands-on approach to watching out for your children."

INFLUENCE THEIR CHOICE OF FRIENDS

One of the more sensitive tasks undertaken by Revolutionary Parents was that of influencing their child's choice of friends. This practice is resented by most children and deemed inappropriate by many parents. Consequently, effective parents engage in this practice cautiously—and quietly.

"I always helped my kids choose their friends—but I think I was able to do it without them realizing it," stated one parent of spiritual champions. "I would never come right out and tell them they could not befriend a particular peer, or outright criticize one of their potential buddies. My approach was always more subtle, based on asking pointed questions about behavior or beliefs that were substantially different from what we allowed."

More than three out of every four Revolutionary Parents admitted to intentionally influencing the friends their children selected. Acknowledging the impact that friends have on their peers, these parents spent enough time with their children and their potential playmates to get a good sense of the companions' family background, the core values they held, and how they interacted in various situations. The parents would strongly encourage relationships with children who seemed like a good match and positive influence, and gently discourage continued involvement with less desirable playmates. Sometimes a more definitive stand was called for, resulting in an outright prohibition against befriending a particular individual. But those confrontations were few and far between. The parent-child connection was strong enough that, in most instances, the parent's advice was accepted and other friends filled the gap.

Do not overlook one of the supplementary advantages of being so closely involved in the lives of your children that you know their friends quite well. This level of intimacy afforded the Revolutionary Parents we interviewed the opportunity to exert positive influence on those friends as well. Several parents recited times when they led their child's friends to Christ or helped them work through personal crises that their own parents did not seem prepared to address. They were not interested in parenting their child's friends, but neither were they shy about sharing their own values and beliefs in an appropriate manner.

“As a Christian parent, I have a responsibility to raise my own children, hopefully with a deep faith in Christ,” explained one parent. “But as a follower of Christ, in general, the world is my mission field. Children are vulnerable to all types of worldly influences. If I have a chance to help them make better choices, how can I turn my back on that opportunity? I always saw those as ‘God moments,’ when the Lord put me in those situations for a reason. Those were not accidents. I could either shy away from those moments out of fear of meddling in the child’s life, or I could see myself as God’s agent doing His will in the best interests of the child. I chose the latter view.”

ESTABLISH MEDIA LIMITS

Children spend more time with the mass media than they spend with anything or anyone else in life. Our most recent surveys show that the typical preteen child devotes an average of more than forty hours per week to ingesting media content.[2] Teens are only slightly less affected by media saturation.

Most parents become willing victims of media manipulation. Even though I do not believe there is a conspiracy by media executives to steal the minds and hearts of children, I do believe that God’s enemies have adopted the media as a means of exposing children to ideas and images that are harmful to their development as servants of God. Frankly, the only effective firewall between our children and such abuse is parents. Parents can significantly affect what media content their children absorb.

There was no single approach used by the bulk of the

Revolutionary Parents when it came to controlling media intake. Some of these families rid their entire household of televisions and other media equipment. Some families allocated media time as a reward for good academic performance. Other families allowed the children to determine their own media diet, within the family's parameters regarding acceptable content (such as no MTV, no NC-17 or R-rated movies, no rap music, and so on).[3] While we encountered a few families in which there were no limits whatsoever to the media choices of their kids, my sense was that this was only because specific rules were not necessary: Their children seemed rather disinterested in much of the content that appealed to their peer group.

One of the insights into what made this work out for Revolutionary Parents was their willingness to explain to their kids the problems embedded in the media content being denied.

"We always watched every movie with our children," remembered a parent of five. "After the movie was completed, we would discuss what was right and wrong in the movie—a kind of worldview lesson. At first they hated the fact that we were 'taking the fun' out of their entertainment experience. After a while, though, they began to see the patterns in those media, and became pretty savvy consumers of films and TV and even music. Eventually, they pretty much lost interest in most of the audiovisual media and spent more time reading and creating their own media. I must admit, it was a real struggle at first, but it became a real blessing to see them understand why we had trouble with the media their generation adored and to see them develop good alternatives."

The spiritual champions who are now adults intimated

in our research that the limitations defined by their parents were a godsend.

"I look at my classmates today and realize how twisted their thinking is, not because they're bad people, but just because they've been exposed to so much garbage without any kind of filter or analysis," was the view of one such young adult. "When we were growing up I envied my friends because their parents allowed them to make their own choices about television and movies and music. It seemed so unfair. And when I was able to watch or listen to stuff, my parents frequently commented on the moral nature of the message in those programs or songs. Man, did I get tired of that! But the proof is in the results. Self-regulation failed with my friends; parental regulation worked wonders for me. Now I feel bad about all the grief I gave my parents about sticking their nose in my business, but what a difference it made. From talking with them about it, I know it was pretty distasteful for them at the time, but they cared enough to do it. I am so grateful."

In fact, the unwillingness of parents to closely monitor and limit media was listed by spiritual champions as a glaring fault of many parents. Giving children the freedom to determine their own media diet was ranked as one of the most insidious weaknesses of today's parents, producing outcomes that will haunt their children—and our society—for years to come.

IF YOU LIVE HERE . . .

Revolutionary Parents make no bones about it: If a child expects to live in their house, the child not only has to abide by their rules, but also has to embrace their values. Rules that are not based on a comprehensive, underlying value system become a modern form of legalism. But rules that stem from values based on a biblical worldview give meaning and purpose to behavior.

I discovered that most Revolutionary Parents embody their Christian values better than they are able to identify them. Perhaps that is a weakness in the system. But it might not be as debilitating as it seems. From my observation of and conversations with these parents, it appears that their core values—love, obedience, servanthood, compassion, grace, good citizenship, humility, respect, and so forth—were consistently put into practice, enabling their budding spiritual champions to pick up those values, whether they were verbalized or not.

It seems that these values were a direct consequence of the constant spiritual growth that the parents sought for themselves. Their regular reading and study of the Scriptures, along with a serious prayer life and engagement in genuine worship, were a vibrant source of such values. The amount of time they invested in growing their faith undoubtedly enabled them to embody the values rather than having to provide sterile, disembodied lectures on the importance of such qualities.

DISAGREEMENT ON DISCIPLINE

There are all kinds of debates that get parents fired up on both ends of the liberal-conservative continuum. One of those relates to forms of discipline. The hottest discipline issue may well be whether a parent should spank a child. One might expect the parents who produced spiritual champions to help settle this debate once and for all. Surprisingly, we learned that Revolutionary Parents simply add fuel to the fire. They were consistent in that they chose a discipline approach and stuck to it, but there was no clear-cut approach of choice within the population of Revolutionary Parents.

The range of options found among these parents was unexpectedly broad. One couple said they recommend using a leather strap on children to enforce discipline. Another parent said neither she nor her husband had ever spanked their children or even raised their voices to them. You can imagine the variations that fell in between.

One conclusion can be drawn, however. Discipline is necessary and fruitful. Both the Revolutionary Parents and their godly children agreed on four aspects of appropriate discipline.

First, the child must constantly receive discipline. Second, the discipline received must be consistent in content and in response to the conditions in which it is provided. Third, the nature of the discipline must fit within the family's culture and values. Fourth, and perhaps the most difficult factor to master, is that the discipline each child receives must be right for that child, while still being fair to the other children in the household. It need not be the same for each child, but each child must be held accountable to the same rules under equivalent conditions.

AMBIVALENCE TOWARD EDUCATION

Exemplary parents expected their children to do their best and to perform at or above their competence level while in elementary and secondary school. Another surprise we received, though, was that parental expectations regarding college ran the gamut.

On the one hand, some Revolutionary Parents went all out to get their children into the best colleges; on the other hand, some demonstrated indifference about whether their son or daughter even chose to apply to a college. This latter approach varied in motivation. Some parents felt their child was not academically inclined and did not want to push him or her into an environment ill-suited to the child. Other parents wanted their youngster to attend college but felt the decision should be made by the child.

A few parents were at odds with their child over the decision—they pushed college, the child fought it—but had chosen not to force their position. (It should be noted that there were more than a few cases where the parent and child differed in preference, and the parents did insist that the child attend college against the child's wishes.)

The fascinating insight related to this battleground is that every one of the children in question wound up loving God and being connected to a community of faith in a dynamic way. Some of these Kingdom stalwarts were on a fast-track career path. Others were filling low-wage temporary jobs. The sense that emerged from our interviews with the young adults was that the ultimate decision about the importance of a college education was more likely to be seen as a defining moment for parents than it was for their children. Many parents had worked hard with their kids to help them perform well academically; attending college was seen as the payoff. Having a child who was capable of attending and succeeding in college but who nevertheless chose not to attend was seen as a defeat. This conflict was perhaps more of a growth moment for the parents than for their young adults.

"To be honest, it broke my heart that Brandon refused to go to college. He was not the most academic of students, but he was certainly bright enough and could have done well in college, if he'd given it a try," rued a mother, forlorn over her son's decision to join the workforce directly out of high school.

"But the Lord has taught me that Brandon's worth is not in the kind of job he has but in the character he demonstrates and in his love for God," she continued. "I've spent a lot of time thinking about my dreams for him and God's dreams for him. I've concluded that if God's will is to be done in Brandon's life, the most important thing is not whether he has a college degree, but whether he serves God. I've come to appreciate the fact—and to thank God for it—that Brandon is a committed follower of Christ and lives in ways that are consistent with our beliefs. I know that pleases God. Having a college degree would have pleased me, but it's more important that he honor the Lord. I've made my peace with this, and now I simply appreciate Brandon's heart for God. I prayed for that for years. When God answered that promise, I just wasn't ready for the way He answered it."

For the spiritual champions themselves, attending college was usually judged on its merits, rather than assumed as the natural outcome for a high school graduate. As young people dedicated to loving and serving God and His people, their life's focus was more spiritual than economic or intellectual. Although they were sensitive to the demands of a first-world economy and the desires of their loving parents, they tended to lean more toward doing that which advanced their spiritual development and experience rather than their career ascension and status.

Rapid Review

- Pick your fights. Not everything merits a confrontation. Be prepared to win your battles.
- Establish clear rules and expectations. You are responsible for establishing guidelines your children can understand and follow.
- Establish and enforce a curfew.
- Participate in the selection of your children's friends. Those peers have a dramatic influence on your children.
- Identify the media regimen you will allow for your children. Limits must be set and enforced, or your kids' media diet will expand according to the time available.
- Empower your children to adopt your morals and values.
- Identify a model of discipline you will use, and deploy it consistently.

Hands-On

1. Track the criticisms, limits, rewards, and punishments you meted out this week. How consistent have you been in dispensing household justice?

2. When your children go someplace without you, insist that they establish verbal contact with you at regular intervals. Merely being accessible is not enough.

3. If you want to know what a friend of your child's is like, size up the parents. Do not allow your child to go to someone's house until you meet the parents or guardians, know their situation, and know a responsible parent will be present.

4. Get used to discussing the moral underpinning of movies and TV shows with your kids. Not only do you train them to think critically about such content, but it gives you insight into what they are and are not sensitive to in media content, and allows you to assess their ability to analyze culture.

chapter six

HOW REVOLUTIONARY PARENTS BEHAVE

EVERYONE HAS A ROLE to fill, whether he or she likes it or not. Each role has expected behavior that accompanies it. Parenting is such a role. There are specific behaviors and responsibilities associated with raising children.

Studying how Revolutionary Parents did their job turned up evidence that they exhibited some of the parenting behaviors you'd expect. It also revealed others that are not as obvious.

WHO'S THE BOSS?

My associates and I have interviewed soldiers who returned from deployment in the Middle East about the factors that were most critical to success on their missions. The soldiers have invariably given answers that relate to leadership: The mission could not succeed unless there was one person in charge who was the acknowledged leader and had the attention and respect of the soldiers involved.

Revolutionary moms and dads must have that same kind of leadership stature with their children. The parents who raised spiritual champions left no doubt in my mind—or in that of their children—that they had control, knew they were in control, and their children recognized that control.

How was that message conveyed to the children? I encountered the following ways:

- Declaring verbally who was in charge and providing frequent reminders
- Acting like the commander
- Accepting the responsibilities and pressures that came with the leadership role
- Earning the appreciation and acknowledgment of the children by meeting their emotional, physical, and spiritual needs; providing such benefits minimized the resistance to parental claims upon leadership
- Strengthening intellectual claims on leadership by anticipating and solving problems, and helping the child mature as a problem solver
- Reinforcing spiritual claims to leadership by presenting biblical principles regarding family roles, including the responsibilities assigned by God to the parents and to children
- Spending time with other families who embraced the same values and beliefs, silently reinforcing the perspectives through external examples

In short, Revolutionary Parents believe they are in charge from day one, behave like people who are in charge, and never allow doubts to linger as to who is in charge. Not all of them like the fact that they are in charge—for some, it is a job they accept with resignation rather than relish—but they all realize that giving their children a hint of their distaste for the job would open the door to constant challenges and conflicts.

Many parents who fail to produce spiritual champions suggest that being a "command and control" type of parent is uncalled for or even counterproductive. They describe such behavior as "over the top," "domineering," "insensitive," "compensation for personal weakness," and "not loving." I shared those thoughts with some of the Revolutionary Parents.

"They're welcome to their opinion," said one mother, sighing. "Just don't bring their children to me when they're teens or in their early twenties, because that's when the stuff will hit the fan. Raise your kids democratically and you'll get kids who live up to the lowest common denominator. Those kids are an amoral and emotional mess," said this Revolutionary Parent. "Children need parents to be strong and in charge—not to the point of crushing their [the children's] spirit or disallowing participation in decision making, but someone who has the final say and takes responsibility for the decisions made. You give kids too much leeway and it becomes chaos. If a parent refuses to be in charge, you get the inmates running the asylum. That's bad in the short run but disastrous over the long run."

Many people who take control of the parenting reins admit that it takes time to get used to the role.

"I'm not a control person by nature," said one mother, "but when you have little ones depending on you for direction, you learn pretty quickly how important it is to be the leader. It's never going to be my comfort zone, but I came to realize that keeping control of your kids comes with the territory. I figured if you could give them birth, then you could—and had to—give them constant guidance. I pushed myself to realize that my time to relax would begin once they were grown and gone. Until that time, it was a daily stretch for me to maintain control of the family without losing my cool or my witness to the kids. It didn't always work, but it worked out fine more times than not."

The ability of most parents to rise to the occasion may reflect more on their children than their own abilities.

"I think I've been able to get away with being the boss because, deep down, the kids want me to be in control," related a father of three. "They will periodically test me to see if I'm still up to the challenge, but the bottom line is they want to have the confidence that the old man is capable of handling the job. Once I prove, over and over, that I can do it and that I intend to retain the leadership role, they can relax and feel as if everything is in balance in their universe. I'm sure there are some kids who live to wrestle control away from their parents and teachers, but in my experience most kids seem content to let the parents rule the roost until an appropriate time later in life when they will be ready to take over on their own."

NO TEMPER TANTRUMS

Nobody argues that it's good for parents to lose their temper, but kids have a way of finding and pushing the emotional buttons of parents, sometimes triggering an overly harsh response. Discipline is one of the most challenging aspects of raising children, and as we saw in the previous chapter, there is no universally accepted formula for it. But one consistent principle that emerged among Revolutionary Parents was their ability to contain their anger and frustration. They got upset with their children but were able to channel their emotions into positive and productive solutions.

Our nationwide studies among all young adults pointed to verbal abuse as one of the most serious mistakes made by parents. Not all parents were guilty of harmful speech, but a surprisingly large number of Baby Busters criticized their parents for saying things that were permanently hurtful.[1] The Bible speaks clearly about the power of words; the lives of America's children are a continuing testimony to the importance of keeping our words in check.

Controlling our words is easier said than done (no pun intended). How did the parents in our study manage to do this? Some said they developed simple habits, such as counting to ten before answering a child in a tense moment. Others got in the practice of saying a brief, silent prayer before responding. A few said that they made it a point to lower both the pitch and the volume of their voices in those situations, which often had an unnerving effect on the children: The youngsters immediately knew they had triggered some serious conflict and that their parent was on edge. A handful of Revolutionary Parents said they firmly reminded their kids of one of several core principles as a means of controlling their own words and breaking the tension. Of course, the principle they chose had a direct correlation to the power struggle at hand.

There was not one particular practice embraced by all or even most of the parents we interviewed to help them watch over their tongues. It seems, however, that the sensitivity of these mothers and fathers to the potential hurt or damage that could be done by a verbal torrent kept their speech under wraps the vast majority of the time.

What about those times—however few—when the parent inappropriately blasted the young one? Again, there was no universal reaction by the successful parents, but the most common response—and the one that seems most biblical—was for the parent to apologize to the child.

Some adults might think of this as a show of weakness, but I believe that children are more likely to appreciate the evidence of the humanness and vulnerability of their parents. In most of the cases we studied, the apology was accompanied with an explanation of why the parent lost control; for example, why the offense was out of line and how it (or the cumulative effect of such shenanigans) finally pushed the parent past the breaking point. While the research did not speak to this, I think offering such an explanation with the apology made the parent seem like a stronger leader: one who cared too much to simply blow up and move on.

A PURPOSE FOR EVERYTHING

Kids are not always logical, but they expect their parents to have logical reasons for everything they do. Parents are not obligated to share that logic with their youngsters, but the extraordinary parents we interviewed noted that they typically included an explanation along with their commands so that the children felt that there was nothing capricious being foisted upon them.

"I think my children learned a lot about their faith and values by my explaining my expectations and disciplinary measures. They didn't always agree with my train of thought or conclusions, and sometimes my explanations instigated conflict, but over the course of time it seemed as if my consistency in my reasoning either wore them down or put them on the defensive," was the view of one great mother who raised her kids in Tennessee. "I think they actually developed a better spiritual sense because they could follow my logic trail and see how I was combining our faith and their behavior."

Such a stance implies that parents have a well-conceived philosophy that directs their efforts and a set of objectives to satisfy through those efforts. For example, we discovered that 73 percent of the Revolutionary Parents placed "a lot of emphasis" upon protecting their children from negative influences. That goal led to measures such as limiting their child's media exposure and assisting in their selection of friends.

The very concept of being purposeful in their parenting efforts generally led the parents to establish and pursue specific and practical goals. Some of the goals were parent-related (such as modeling certain values or behaviors, or praying daily for the child). Other goals were set for the child to accomplish (for example, developing a solid sense of right and wrong, or displaying commitment to fulfilling obligations). The goals we discovered covered a wide range of life dimensions, but the common thread was that great parents saw potential value in goal setting—and to the present day believe that this practice was instrumental in the success they achieved.

An interesting side note is that purposeful behavior by parents often entailed personal sacrifice. The most significant of those perhaps was the parents' willingness to give up experiences they would have liked to have had.

One mother remembered how stunned she was in the beginning of her parenting era to have to retool her existence. "Once the kids reached the walking-talking stage, I went into shock because I couldn't continue doing all the things I was accustomed to doing. Hobbies were no longer possible. The simple pleasures—like watching a favorite TV show uninterrupted every morning or going shopping with my girlfriends one morning a week—those were gone, too. At first I resented the radical change in my life, but then I recognized that I had wanted to have children and this was part of the bargain. Giving up your own needs is part of being a good parent. The initial anger about it was really just my own selfishness showing through. It was good to realize how much I could surrender if I needed to. That insight helped me to grow in my faith, as I began to see other areas of my life that needed greater surrender in order for me to grow and become more like Jesus. I actually came to realize that it wasn't so much that I lost everything—that I had no life—but that now I had a very different life that could be just as rich and rewarding if I let it."

It wasn't just mothers who made sacrifices for the good of their children; Revolutionary fathers did so as well. Whether it was their refusal to pursue occupational advancement because of the time and travel demands or not participating in sports leagues or professional organizations because of their time commitments, the willingness to prioritize the family was a hallmark of fathers who were intent upon raising spiritual champions.

Our research revealed a synergy between the philosophy underlying the parenting effort, the goals that were set to facilitate great outcomes, and the recognition that surrender was required to foster the desired results. My sense was that this wisdom usually took a lot of time and experimentation before the connection became clear and acceptable. Great parents typically grow into that mold; it does not come naturally, and the values upheld in popular culture make it even more difficult. However, the unwavering focus on the quality of their child's heart and soul enabled the parents we studied to put the pieces together in a way that allowed both parent and child to mature in tandem.

THE OPEN DOOR–OPEN EAR POLICY

One of the most harmful ideals to grip the minds of parents over the past two decades is that of "quality time." A majority of parents across the nation have swapped the idea of committing significant amounts of time to spend with their children for the notion that it doesn't matter how much—or how little—time they allocate to their relationship with their children because the important factor is the quality of the time spent with them.

Millions of parents have accepted the idea that they have to make a choice. They must either give up careers and self-fulfillment and spend a lot of time with their children, or spend limited but deeply enriching time with them while maintaining the same level of vocational involvement. Over the past fifteen years, various studies have shown that this switch has diminished the impact of parents. And the lie about the choice involved has hurt both parents and children, leaving a large proportion of young adults feeling as if they were not adequately parented and a shockingly high number feeling that they lacked a father figure in their lives. In fact, when we asked young adults what they felt were the most significant mistakes that America's parents have made, the second highest–ranked mistake was not spending enough time with their children. (The failure to provide appropriate discipline was the top-ranked deficiency.)

The Revolutionary Parents we studied somehow rejected the cultural spin and remained true to the commitment to spend a lot of time with their children and also to have special times of intense focus and memorable experiences with their children. When we asked how this worked, we found that most of these parents did not perceive the issue to be one of time, as important as that was, but a combination of factors that determined how the time was used. Some of the most prolific perspectives they shared follow:

- *Highly engaged.* Great parents saw themselves as parents rather than friends of their child, maintaining a highly responsible role during their interaction—precluding the practice of simply being physically present but emotionally or intellectually absent during their times together.
- *Investing time.* They understood that unless they invested substantial amounts of time into the relationship, they would not have a deep relationship with their child—which thus would minimize the potential for lasting influence.
- *Willing to listen.* In the course of spending time with the child, the most important skill was listening to what the child said. It was widely felt by extraordinary parents that too many moms and dads are so busy completing their agendas that they do not hear what's on the minds of their children, and thus miss great opportunities to connect at a deeper level and to take advantage of the life-changing moments being offered by their young ones. Listening is not only the most vital aspect of effective communication, but it serves as a window into the mind and heart of the child—an indispensable chance to get right to the core of the child's needs and growth potential with a minimum of trial and error.
- *Balancing soft and hard.* To make the most of the parent-child experience, Revolutionary Parents described seeking to reach a balance of openness and vulnerability along with

being the authoritative coach. Being too soft and touchy-feely was thought to dampen their potential leadership; being too strong and directive could break the child's spirit or disrupt the relationship. Finding the sweet spot in between the extremes was said to be a difficult journey but one worth the effort.

LIVING THE LIFE

One of the essential child-rearing behaviors identified by the parents of spiritual champions—and confirmed as critically important by the spiritual champions themselves—was the modeling of the principles upheld by the parents. Various studies and researchers have tried to estimate the importance of learning through modeling, producing a vast array of results, but it seems likely that somewhere around 60 percent of the learning that affects people's behavior is based upon watching someone they know and trust doing something significant. This makes particular sense these days, with the built-in hypocrisy detectors that children seem to be born with as standard equipment.

Modeling takes many forms. Our probing with the Revolutionary Parents in the study produced a long list of endeavors that they engaged in as a means of modeling the lifestyle and mind-set they desired for their children. The most common of those modeling exercises boiled down to just three.

- *Respect.* Children might push back when disciplined, but they expect parents to provide correction and guidance.

The key, according to both the Revolutionary Parents and the transformed children, is for parents to give their input with respect for the child. That does not mean kowtowing to the children's whims; it simply means treating the child with dignity and fairness.

"My parents always treated us with respect—not necessarily like adults, but as human beings who were made in God's image and therefore deserved to be treated with sensitivity and kindness," recalled one of the transformed young adults. "It really made me listen to them more closely and give them the benefit of the doubt more often, especially when I compared how they treated me with how my friends' parents treated them. I could not have explained it at the time, but I think I felt kind of honored that they would treat me so wonderfully. I think some of my friends were pretty jealous of it, too."

- *Patience.* Every great parent confessed to struggling with impatience. But more than nine out of ten of them listed patience as one of the necessities in successful parenting. None of them claimed to have mastered the art.

  "No matter how hard I tried," admitted one father, "they always found some way to push me over the edge. I got mellower as they aged, but I had to develop little tricks to hold myself in check."

  Many Revolutionary Parents mentioned finding tricks or other techniques as crucial aids toward maintaining their cool under pressure.

- *Love.* This may be the most used and least understood word in the English vocabulary. The way that transformational parents interpreted it was as a hands-on demonstration of care—not a gooey emotion or feeling of affection. Children need to know that their parents will do whatever it takes to accept, nurture, and protect them. That is typically what they seek as "love."

  One parent put it well: "Children reflect what they see and what they aspire to be from among the options that they see. I knew they had a lot of choices, but I wanted to be the best option for them to imitate. Every day I thought about what I could and would do to persuade them that what I was teaching them was their best alternative. It was hard work, but it paid off."

RELIABILITY RULES

Consistency alone is not enough to raise a spiritual champion, but the absence of consistency in discipline, values, expectations, beliefs, and modeling can easily be the undoing of the parent. We heard this often from adult children: Those who are spiritual champions today attributed it partially to the consistency of their parents' efforts, and young adults who are not living a transformed life today frequently noted that their parents lacked consistency.

The most common consideration in this regard deals with following through on rules and standards. Parents must give children the rules, the rules must be enforced consistently, and there must be consequences for the failure to stay in line. The failure to follow through on those expectations makes a shambles of the parents' authority and their ability to keep youngsters on track.

Of course, sometimes parents have to alter the parameters they have set up, realizing that what they are doing simply is not working as planned. Change is not a big deal; but change without communication causes problems. When the parameters change without explanation or a connection to reality, children become confused and eventually assume that the rules are capricious and therefore unworthy of compliance. The Revolutionary Parents concurred that shifting away from inefficient standards can be done effectively if the parent explains to the child why the change is required and how the new standard will be defined and applied. Such changes are then made in context, and the child is more likely to be responsive.

APPROVED BY GOD

One of the nonnegotiable factors imbedded within the parenting behaviors of the great parents was their insistence on faith in God and obedience to biblical principles as the driving force behind the household culture and their child-rearing practices.

Unlike most American parents who deem themselves to be Christian, Revolutionary Parents earnestly accept the role of being the primary and dominant spiritual mentor of their children. Most of them acknowledge the importance of being active in a healthy community of faith, but they also define that community's role as one of supplementing what the parents are doing. Transformational parenting entails adopting a leadership position when it comes to fostering a child's faith; leaving the job to the religious professionals is an inappropriate transfer of authority and power to people and organizations that God never intended.

We learned that, in the process of nurturing a spiritual champion, parents enhance transformation by praying daily for the spiritual development of their children and by taking time to read and discuss the Bible together.

While it might be ideal to engage in such Bible study every day, we found that few parents in our research did so; they were more likely to deal with Bible content once or twice a week (excluding times when they were at church together). Many parents who raised spiritual champions did not have a stringent or organized scriptural trail they were following in the journey they took with their children. Often these parents would select Bible passages that addressed a specific incident or event that made God's Word relevant to their kids.

"I tried doing devotionals with the kids, and even Bible studies, sometimes using printed guidebooks for each of us," lamented one father. "It never clicked. We finally took a step of faith and simply chose portions of the Scriptures that seemed most closely related to what one of us was going through and tried to get our kids used to turning to the Word for wisdom. Thank God, it developed into a habit for all of them, and even today they are pretty regular about checking the Bible for guidance as things come up."

The practice of prayer is too frequently overlooked by parents. Revolutionary Parenting incorporates every tool at the disposal of the parent. Prayer is one of the most powerful.

"I cannot tell you how much strength I got from my daily prayers about the children," a retired mother of two Revolutionaries said, beaming. "God hears and He responds. He heard me and He helped me. Every parent should tap into that power of the Lord as they raise their children. It's a mighty tough task. God wants to help. Prayer is our communication line with Him, and we should use it whenever possible."

Rapid Review

- You are in charge of the family. That must be the undisputed truth in the minds of all residents of your household. You cannot allow the kids to challenge or mock your authority.
- Always keep your emotions under control. Never let your anger take over.
- When children ask for an explanation of your decisions or reasoning, give it to them. They deserve it, and it becomes a teaching moment for you.
- Don't shortcut your role by trying to deliver "quality time" without "quantity time" as well. Always invest

ample time in your relationship and duties with your children.

- Model the principles and behaviors you want the kids to adopt.
- Be consistent. Nothing undermines your efforts like waffling or changing gears.
- Take on the role of spiritual mentor with enthusiasm and expectation.

Hands-On

1. Revolutionary Parents anticipate what's coming. Know that your children will frequently ask why you've made a decision. Be ready for those questions. The more articulate you are, the better the teaching moment.
2. Look at your schedule for the past month. How many times have you blocked out time for a family experience? Make a habit of intentionally scheduling special times together.
3. When you enforce a rule, make sure the consequence is enforced as well. Otherwise, your rules lose their power.
4. Talk with your kids about what they perceive God to be like. As their spiritual mentor, realize that if they do not have a healthy perspective of God, they will not build a healthy faith.

5. Pray throughout the day with the kids: at meals, on the way to school, before sports events, at bedtime, and at any other moment of significance. The more used to weaving God into their lives your children become, the more likely they will retain prayer as a lifelong habit.

A REVOLUTIONARY FAITH

PARENTS WHO RAISE spiritual champions lay a strong foundation for their efforts. They have a comprehensive philosophy of parenting, a clear sense of life priorities, a body of nonnegotiable principles, and the self-discipline to stay focused and energized despite the unforeseen challenges that arise daily. There is one more component of the foundation that we have not directly addressed, and it may be the most important: their spiritual moorings.

One of the impressive traits of Revolutionary Parents is that they integrate their faith into their lives more seamlessly than most people. That integration enables them to make spur-of-the-moment decisions consistent with who they are and who they are trying to develop their children into becoming. The absorption of their Christian faith into every dimension of their life also makes the transfer of the critical perspectives and principles a more natural process for them.

Revolutionary Parents tend to be conservative theologically, which is not surprising since the definition of a spiritual champion is someone who centers life around the person and principles of God. Let me describe some elements of their spiritual base that serve them well.

FAITH IS THE FOUNDATION

Most Americans (84 percent of all adults) claim they are Christian. However, our research clearly delineates different types of Christians.

There are *Revolutionaries*: People for whom God is their priority in life, and everything they do stems from their perception that they live only to love, obey, and serve God. There are *evangelical Christians*, many of whom are Revolutionary in their perspective, and all of whom engage in spreading the gospel of Christ and adopting an orthodox view of the Scriptures. There are *nonevangelical born-again Christians*, who have confessed their sinfulness to God and sought His forgiveness through Christ, but whose interpretations of the Bible and commitment to thoroughly practice its admonitions are spotty. And there are *notional Christians*—those who think of themselves as Christian but are not deeply spiritual and do not have a life-changing relationship with Jesus Christ. Their commitment is more to being religious than it is to being transformed by Christ and living differently because of that faith.[1]

Revolutionary Parents tend to come from among the first three groups mentioned above. We found very few parents who are theologically liberal or spiritually complacent among the parents who raise spiritual champions. While that is not surprising, it reinforces the necessity of parents having the spiritual goods to pass along to their children. Raising a spiritual champion does not happen, as the saying goes, by drinking the water.

More specifically, what this means is that parents are more likely to raise spiritual champions if they

- Genuinely love God
- Pray daily
- Worship regularly
- Read the Bible habitually for personal development
- Participate in the life of a spiritual community
- Apply their resources, spiritual gifts, and natural abilities frequently to influencing lives

One observation from our interviews might also help. These Revolutionary Parents use a lot of "God talk"—not empty phrases, but a genuine intermingling of their relationship with God and their daily experiences and choices. This does not mean that these parents are aggressive evangelists. It does suggest that they see life through a spiritual lens of sorts, and they naturally combine their spiritual perspectives with their descriptions and prescriptions of life.

THE BIBLE IS THE SOURCE

Every parent has a basis on which he or she makes choices about life and parenting. The Revolutionary Parents we studied relied upon the Bible as their primary source of wisdom for life. These were not necessarily "Bible thumpers," who are so often caricatured in the media or by liberal politicians. They were reflective students of God's words, typically reading and thinking about the content of biblical passages several times each week. Many of them admitted that they struggle to understand the meaning of some of the things they read in the Bible but were comfortable with the notion that the Bible is true and accurate in its teachings, whether they can comprehend those insights or not.

These were parents who went beyond trusting the Bible for personal guidance. They spent time reading and talking about that content with their family members, making study of the Scriptures a family routine. This was above and beyond their personal study time. It was perceived by most of these parents to be a critical shaping time for their children's lives and something that defined their family's uniqueness.

"My kids didn't always appreciate the time we put into studying the Bible," said one mother. "But that was something that wasn't up for discussion; we did it, and that was that. Now they thank me for it, and see the value it brought to their life, but at the time, it was not easy. You'd be amazed at the excuses they would come up with when it was time for the family to study the Word."

The purpose of studying the Bible with their children seemed to be the following:

- First, it was intended to teach a child that the best place to search for answers in life is in God's instructions to us.
- Second, by turning to the Bible consistently, the hope was

that each child would adopt the idea that there are truth principles that must be integrated into life; decision making on the fly or based on feelings is inappropriate.

- Third, a number of parents spoke about modeling the value of studying the Scriptures in the company of others and benefiting from the group's wisdom.
- Finally, there was the hope that regular exposure to God's principles would begin to build a worldview that would serve their children well for the duration of their lives.

ABSOLUTE MORAL TRUTH MATTERS

Not all of the Revolutionary Parents we spoke to possessed a biblical worldview. However, a much higher proportion than normal did—more than three times the national average. And a majority of these parents—compared to less than one-quarter of other parents—believe that absolute moral truth exists.

While it is not possible to know exactly how the belief in absolute moral truth affected the day-to-day child-rearing tasks, our conversations with these parents made it clear that they often made a point of contrasting right and wrong for their kids—and that those choices hinged on biblical perspectives. Their approach to discipline also related to the exercise of those moral truths: Choosing when to discipline their children, and the appropriate responses and punishments, was drawn from their perception of God's ways.

A few of the parents whose children had attended public

schools recalled facing occasional battles with teachers and administrators over specific content being taught in the classroom. Besides some of the high-profile skirmishes that have become common across the land—such as teaching related to evolution, sexual responsibility, and marriage—parents identified other issues that moved them to respond. The bottom line in this regard is that great parents are involved enough in their child's world that they know when errant perspectives are being taught as truth or fact—and care deeply and are self-confident enough to confront those who are perpetrating the undesired points of view.

THE CHURCH IS THE VILLAGE

Unlike parents who embrace the "dump and run" strategy of spiritual nurturing—dump the kids at church, run off until the allotted time has expired, then wait until next week to repeat the process to provide their offspring with their dose of spiritual experience—Revolutionary Parents see their church as an invaluable partner in a long-term effort to raise a mature follower of Christ.

"My church was not really responsible for who John [her son] became as a man of God," explained a mother whose son is now an elder in his church and regularly leads short-term missions trips to third-world nations. "But John would not be who he is today if it were not for the work of our church. They truly came alongside my husband and me and helped us to raise a son who loves God. I doubt that would have happened without the support and guidance of our church."

What exactly do these parents look to their faith community to provide in the parenting process? There are some components that focus on the parents, and some that focus on the children. For instance, they rely upon their faith communities to provide them with emotional support through difficult times; relationships with other parents who share their faith commitment and can offer some perspective or fresh ideas; and the spiritual nurturing and motivation they need to keep themselves growing in their relationship with God.

These parents expect their church to reinforce what they are teaching and modeling on the home front. That amplification of biblical principles and lifestyle choices—coming from both home and church—becomes a powerful one-two punch in the parents' assault on the world's alternatives.

"A lot of times we would say something, and it seemed to go in one ear and out the other," said one mom, laughing in retrospect. "But when her youth leader would say the same things we'd been harping on at home, [our daughter would] come back with her jaw hanging, as if she had just discovered that we weren't the antiquated, oddball parents she had assumed us to be. The affirmation we received from the good teaching at church was very helpful to us."

Another value of these spiritual communities is their ability to connect children to friends more likely to have biblical morals and parents who take such matters seriously.

"Our church had some kids in the youth group that I didn't care for and didn't want our kids to spend time with," admitted a mother of two children who grew up to be spiritual champions. "But on the whole, the kids there were better quality than the others they were exposed to in the schools. At least with their friends from church you had a foundation of Christianity to build on. My husband and I still had to sift through our children's friends carefully, but we had better experiences with the church friends than with the others they encountered."

The local church also provides help to the family in terms of creating opportunities to grow spiritually by serving others and by worshipping in the presence of others. "We tried a few times to worship God as a family, at home, but it never clicked for us. At least at church they developed the habit of worshipping God regularly and came to enjoy it."

LOVE IS THE METHOD

Interviewing the parents of these spiritual champions confirmed something that the grown children mentioned: Their parents loved them into the presence of God.

"I wasn't exactly an angel when I was an adolescent," recalled one of the spiritual champions. "But my parents, especially my mom, just loved me so much that her love alone forced me to change. Maybe subconsciously I equated her love with God's, but in college, when I had psych courses, I began to realize that her love was a reflection of the even deeper love that God has for me. It was not just something that got me through my childhood, but a love that made all the church talk about the love of God a very real thing for me."

Love is apparently more than just a theological concept to great parents. It serves as both a reflection of their own gratitude for what God has done for them personally as well as a means of transferring that love into the lives of their young ones.

Many of the parents used the Christian term *unconditional love* to describe their objective.

"On those days when I felt more like killing my daughter than loving her—because of her mouth or attitude or whatever—I was often drawn back to the thought that this must be what it's like for God to put up with my sins," a mother told us. "His response was to die for me. Remembering that always—well, usually—helped me to stay centered and to respond in a more calm and loving way to my daughter—at least, more calm and loving than I was feeling. If God could love me unconditionally, I was determined to try to love my kids the same way. I failed a lot, but I sure did a whole lot better because of that ideal."

In practical terms, unconditional love was interpreted by these parents as continually assuring their children that whatever the parent was doing was being done out of love for the child. Sometimes that was a harder sell than at other times, but the parents' consistent demonstration of love eventually penetrated their children's consciousness. That assurance made it easier for the parents to discipline their children, who accepted the punishment with the understanding that they were still accepted and appreciated by the family despite their transgressions.

"In Danielle's case," reflected a father who is not naturally confrontational but who regularly disciplined his daughter, "the almost nagging reminders from me and my wife that we really did love her seemed to get through to her when she was in her early teens. I think it was then that she connected our efforts to discipline her as one example of how much we loved her. And then she seemed to connect the dots between our continual love of her, despite the rules and punishments and limits, with the depth of God's love for her. It was very special, but it sure didn't happen overnight."

MAKING A CHOICE FOR CHRIST

One of the intriguing strategies of these parents was that despite their steadfast commitment to honor God and to do everything they could to raise godly children, their dominant goal was not to get their child "saved." Every one of these parents considered the salvation of their children to be of paramount importance, but most of them opted for a lifelong emphasis upon discipleship rather than evangelism.

Christians, in general, are of two distinct schools of thought on this matter. One group believes that there is nothing more important than being saved, and thus these parents place their resources into achieving that outcome, usually indicated by the child saying some type of prayer requesting God's forgiveness and indwelling. The other group stresses the importance of children making an informed decision to follow Christ based on their knowledgeable willingness to change their lives in order to obey and serve God. The ideal stance may be a combination of both, but the bottom line is that evangelism without discipleship is spiritual abuse.

The great parents we studied typically waited for their children to make the decision to pursue Christ as their Savior, preparing them for that choice by educating them about the

Christian faith and demonstrating what it looks like in practice. The most impressive facet of this process was the amount of prayer that these parents invested in their children's future spiritual standing. If anything, it seemed that they prayed their children into the Kingdom of God. These parents consistently brought the salvation of their young ones before God but did not pressure their kids to make that choice.

"It was one of those testing times," one father said when asked to describe what it was like waiting for his son to embrace Jesus. "I probably could have argued with him and backed him into heaven, but then it would not have been his decision, it would have been Dad imposing his will on his son. I knew this had to be his choice so that he'd stick with it. Man, it took forever! We kept praying, teaching, going to church, discussing moral and spiritual issues, the whole shot. Finally, at the end of junior high, he proudly told us that he had made up his mind, and Jesus was the way. We were ecstatic, of course, but there were a lot of sleepless nights leading up to that. But I'd do it the same way again. It has to be the child's choice, not one he's pressed into. We tried to live in a way that made that choice attractive, and naturally we had our downfalls, but God was gracious in pursuing him."

A SERVICE MIND-SET

One of the insights gleaned from years and years of research among Christians is that you do not learn to serve others unless you get your eyes off yourself long enough to see the needs of others and the heart of God. In our society, shifting our gaze from ourselves to others is countercultural. Importantly, the parents we interviewed recognized the necessity of developing the habit of serving others and sought ways of inculcating that in their children's lives.

The means of serving seems to morph as a child ages. In the younger years, many of these parents had their children perform simple acts of pragmatic service: cutting the lawn of an elderly widow, taking care of the neighbors' dog for free when they went away, doing nice things for sick classmates. As the children aged, the acts of service shifted to endeavors with a more overtly spiritual bent, such as joining a short-term mission team or visiting elderly adults in retirement homes or care centers.

Another key to making the servant mentality stick was to have the entire family participate in such efforts on a regular basis. This was not necessarily a weekly routine, but these families joined together to meet needs often enough that it became part of the family's identity. The parents noted that this was often a prime time to teach spiritual principles while operating in the trenches. Sometimes the children resisted because serving people clearly set them apart from the crowd.

"Jessica complained about having to join us in working down at the homeless shelter once a month," said one mom. "She kept reminding us that none of her friends had to do that. But I can honestly say that directly after we'd spend a few hours with the poor, she was more teachable than any other time. Something about being around people in such desperate need really got through to her. It gave me and my husband opportunities to encourage her for her sacrifice and to tie the experience to a biblical life principle."

A PREMIUM PLACED ON PRAYER

I could not accurately profile the heart and soul of Revolutionary Parents without emphasizing the premium they place on prayer. This stems from their conviction that God hears and answers all prayers. These are parents who believe their greatest source of power and hope is God, and prayer is the channel that delivers it.

One of the secrets to transformational parenting is not only telling God your dreams for your children and the challenges they face—after all, He already knows that—but actively seeking His response. Sometimes that might be through "open doors" and other times through a Scripture passage that is so relevant to your situation that it blows your mind. But God sometimes will impress His will upon your mind and heart, if you are sensitive to that communiqué. The research indicates that many of the great parents we interviewed were eager to hear from God and waited until He spoke to them in whatever way He chose.

No matter what approach these parents took to prayer, please recognize how central prayer was in their parenting. Most of these parents prayed daily for each of their children, asking God to care for them in ways specific to the child and his or her needs.

Rapid Review

- You can't pass on what you don't possess, so be sure you have a vibrant relationship with God. Pursue Him and practice good spiritual habits.
- Regard the Bible as your guidebook. Trust it and rely on it in all circumstances.
- Embrace the existence and significance of absolute moral truths revealed by God.
- Be active in a community of faith.
- Never push salvation on your children. Lead them toward Christ, encourage them to accept Him, but allow the decision to be theirs.
- Serve other people with your children.
- Pray regularly, openly, and faithfully.

Hands-On

1. Never be embarrassed to let your children see your faith in process and in practice. They learn by observing and imitating. Give them something worth mimicking.
2. Make a list of the critical principles you want your children to adopt from Scripture. Plan how you will study the Bible together to get those principles before them.
3. When opportunities arise, challenge your kids to defend their position on moral truth. Be prepared to explain your position, with scriptural support.

4. Invite some of your children's friends from your church's children's or youth group over to your house. Encourage church-based relationships to flourish.
5. Pray every morning and every evening for the salvation and spiritual maturity of your children. It's a battle for their souls. Your prayers are the ammunition.
6. When your prayers are answered, be sure to mention that to your children and to give God the credit. You don't have to go overboard. If you're sensitive to the working of God in your life, the examples will be plentiful and remarkable enough that you don't have to force the case.

chapter eight

TRAINING UP SPIRITUAL CHAMPIONS

IF YOU DON'T KNOW where you're going, then any road will get you there. Ambiguity regarding destination, however, was not one of the characteristics of most Revolutionary Parents we interviewed. They came from a range of backgrounds and had diverse levels of educational achievement, but they tended to believe in the power of planning for the future. Their plans were based upon specific goals they sought to achieve in their parenting efforts.

There were, of course, two distinct types of goals: those for themselves (which we have touched upon in previous chapters as we have moved through the research results) and those relevant to their children. The goals for their children were taken seriously as soon as their children began their formal school experience—usually around age five.

Most of the parents who set goals involved their children

in the process of choosing the goals as well as the means of accountability associated with them.

"Their participation in the process really helps them to feel some ownership of the goals," recalled one mother. "We tried imposing the goals and it just didn't work as well as conceiving them together."

The types of goals the children had the greatest influence upon included their grades, household chores, behavioral standards, and Bible reading.

FORMING THE MIND

American parents are nearly unanimous in their efforts to help their children make better decisions in life: 96 percent say they are involved in that adventure. Not surprisingly, most parents think they do a good job at facilitating this capability among their children.

The Revolutionary Parents in our research seemed to approach the task a bit differently, however. Their aim was to teach their children how to think independently, basing their choices on core principles and building upon those perspectives to take account of the context and possibilities. A significant element in that process was the willingness to challenge assumptions and statements of fact.

Training their children to question everything—"within reason," we were assured—was designed as a defense against the cultural assault of postmodernism.

"When teachers make blanket statements about the way things are—whether it relates to evolution, gender roles, or the basis of truth—I cannot be there to screen my kids from wrong thinking. So I have to make sure they have been sensitized to ways of thinking that are at odds with what we believe and what we stand for. I want a little red flag to pop up in their head, and for them to make sure they're not accepting statements as facts that are simply not accurate," explained a mother of two spiritual champions. "With one of our children we did not start that process until she was beginning high school. It helped, but it was a struggle because we started so late. It was a brand-new way of thinking for her, and it caused a lot of discomfort for her, emotionally and intellectually. With our younger son, we started the process when he was still in elementary school, so by the time he reached high school, it was a natural thing for him to do."

Raising independent thinkers can create both chaos and occasional anarchy within the home if the limitations are not clarified at the beginning of the process.

"Some parents I know have kids who are out of control because they have told their kids that everything is fair game—nothing is out of bounds when it comes to discerning truth," reflected a father in the Midwest whose boys have grown to become leaders in their church and show evidence of continuing the Revolutionary Parenting tradition with their own youngsters. "From day one we established that some things can be examined but not really questioned. The preeminence of God. Parental authority. Civic duty. Marital fidelity. Those kinds of things. They needed to know that we encourage creative thought, but that there are some boundaries that cannot be violated without serious negative consequences. Those boundaries are set by God, not man, which made it a bit easier for us to impose. We found you just have to let them know the limitations in life and help them to deal with it."

THE FATIGUE FACTOR

Surveys have shown that one of the major points of stress for children these days is their packed schedules. Our surveys have found that stress levels among adolescents and teens match those of adults. Kids admit to feeling overwhelmed by the quantity of responsibilities thrust upon them, from homework to sports, music lessons to church events, household chores to relational expectations, media intake to hobbies. Parents, who are often more driven to optimize their children's potential than the children themselves, often justify the excessive scheduling as part of "rounding out" the child's experiences. In some cases it is designed to give the child opportunities that the parents never had when they were young. Whatever the ultimate motivation, wrapped up in the phenomenon of schedule stuffing is the notion of getting ahead in the world regardless of what it takes to get there.

It was surprising to find how many Revolutionary Parents were aware of the importance of protecting their children from burnout. Many of them spoke about having to prioritize competing opportunities and interests so that their youngsters would not suffer from avoidable and unnecessary fatigue.

"I wanted my kids to have lots of experiences and to develop the discipline to pursue excellence in what they did, but I did not want to put too much pressure on them to achieve in a wide range of activities," said one mother, who admitted that she and her husband had to hold themselves back sometimes so that their children could recharge their batteries. "We saw all the options and recognized the value they could bring to our children, but we had to restrain ourselves so that the kids could lead a normal life. They helped choose what they got involved in, and we simply expected them to do their best and keep striving to do better."

The spiritual-champion children themselves grew up to appreciate the fact that their parents did not overdo it.

"At the time, I was probably a bit ticked that Mom and Dad didn't let me do it all," recalled a young professional. "But in retrospect, I think they were very wise in selecting a handful of activities and asking me to go deep rather than broad. I benefited greatly from the idea of excelling in one or two areas rather than skimming the surface in a dozen. I expect to use that same plan with my kids someday."

SPIRITUAL STANDARDS TO REACH

The spiritual goals that these great parents set for their kids were what you might expect.

Spiritual growth tools. First, they desired their children to develop critical skills pertaining to their faith. The hope was that their kids would know what tools were available for spiritual growth, and they would be experienced and comfortable in using those tools.

The skills they emphasized most often had to do with teaching their children how to pray, how to study the Bible, and how to worship. There was somewhat less emphasis upon sharing one's faith. The skills stressed least often by these parents were knowing their spiritual gifts, developing habits related to service, becoming good stewards of resources, and developing a sense of spiritual community.

Knowledge of other faiths. Second, these were parents who were determined to have their children well educated about different faith groups so they could make an informed choice as to their preferred faith and so they would be better able to defend their faith in conversation with people from other backgrounds. As many of these parents were seeking to help their children develop a biblical worldview, exposure to competing belief systems became a vital part of the educational process.

Foundational Christian teaching. Third, Revolutionary Parents typically worked on enabling their children to grasp critical beliefs related to the Christian faith. The grown children and their parents identified a wide range of tenets that comprised the major beliefs proposed to the young people. There was general agreement that not only were these doctrines and theological views taught, but they were also connected to life outcomes for the children to embrace. The dominant biblical teachings shared with the eventual spiritual champions included the following:

- The Creation story (Genesis 1–2)
- The seduction of Adam and Eve (Genesis 3)
- Moses and the burning bush and Promised Land (Exodus 3)
- Moses and the plagues (Exodus 5–12)

- Moses and the Exodus (Exodus 12–14)
- The Ten Commandments (Exodus 19–20)
- David and Goliath (1 Samuel 16–17)
- Solomon's rise and fall (1 Kings 9–11)
- Job's testing (Job)
- The meaning of life (Ecclesiastes 3, 12)
- Surviving the furnace (Daniel 3)
- Surviving the lions' den (Daniel 6)
- Jonah and the great fish (Jonah)
- The temptations of Christ (Matthew 4:1-11)
- Prayer (Matthew 6:5-15)
- Judging people (Matthew 7:1-6)
- The "Golden Rule" (Matthew 7:12)
- Wealth and salvation (Matthew 19:16-30)
- Servanthood (Matthew 20:20-28)
- Chasing out the money changers (Matthew 21:12-13)
- The greatest commandment (Matthew 22:34-40)
- The Last Supper (Matthew 26:17-30)
- Jesus' crucifixion (Matthew 27:32-56)
- Jesus' resurrection (Matthew 27:57–28:15)
- The great commission (Matthew 28:16-20)
- The birth of Christ (Luke 1–2)
- The Good Samaritan (Luke 10:25-37)
- Nicodemus and salvation (John 3:1-21)
- The ascension of Christ (Acts 1:6-11)
- The coming of the Holy Spirit (Acts 2:1-13)
- The early church (Acts 2)
- Saul's conversion (Acts 9:1-30)
- Falling short (Romans 3:9-31)

- The wages of sin (Romans 6:23)
- Spiritual gifts (1 Corinthians 12)
- Love (1 Corinthians 13)
- The fruit of the Spirit (Galatians 5:22-23)
- Faith in God (Hebrews 11)
- Faith and deeds (James 1–2)

This list is interesting in the breadth of biblical principles it delivers. But just as interesting are the passages that did not make the cut. Think about the myriad of renowned narratives that were not included. Some that come to mind: Noah and the ark; Abraham preparing to kill his son on the altar; Joseph reconnecting with his family; Samson destroying the pagan temple; David and Bathsheba; Solomon building the Temple; Joshua marching around the walls of Jericho; Elijah calling down fire from the heavens; Jesus walking on water or feeding the crowds; and even Paul's three missionary journeys.

While a few of these were mentioned by one or two of the Revolutionary Parents, these stories were not among the significant cornerstones of the training received by the spiritual champions. Only a few parents alluded to why such esteemed and famous sections were missing. One indicated that it was an intentional choice.

"Those are important parts of the Bible, no question about it," admitted one father of a spiritual champion. "But just in terms of teaching fundamental lessons of the faith, they are not as significant as some of the other portions

I mentioned. Don't get me wrong, our children were taught those parts of the Bible and they respect all of the Bible as true and accurate. But if you ask me—as you did—what are the key parts in teaching children to be real followers of God, there are many other parts that offer more central guidance to the Christian life."

The grown children reinforced the value of having been exposed to the core principles their parents taught.

"There was a lot of overlap between what I learned at home and at church," confided a twenty-six-year-old medical school student who is also serving as chaplain of his class. "I'm not a theologian, by any stretch, but my folks did a really good job of building a strong base of Bible knowledge with me and my sisters. They focused on connecting the truth principles from the different stories so that we could relate those insights to what we were doing in our lives. If I had just had the teaching from church, I don't think it would have penetrated nearly as deeply or made such a profound impact on my life. Watching my parents practice what they taught us really drove the lessons home."

In summary, Revolutionary Parents perhaps took greater care than most in creating and tracking goals regarding spiritual development. But those goals were pursued in the context of the type of child they hoped to raise: one who always did his or her best, who thought carefully and aggressively about truth and appropriate living, and who attempted to honor God and family in everything he or she did. The evidence shows that these parents finished well.

Rapid Review

- Teach your children to think independently, based on appropriate principles.
- Be careful that you do not burden your kids with too much activity and responsibility. Just like adults, they can burn out or crack under the stress.
- Help them learn important faith skills, such as prayer, Bible study, and worship.
- Explore different faiths with your children, pointing out similarities and differences.
- Teach your kids the central beliefs and principles of Christianity, using stories and teachings that have personal and practical applications.

Hands-On

1. Talk to your children about whether they feel too much pressure because they don't have time to complete and enjoy tasks. Make adjustments accordingly.
2. Teach your children to respect other faiths. They do not have to accept them as true, but they must respect people's right to pursue their own faith preferences.
3. Develop a list of the faith principles that you believe are critical for your children to learn. Figure out how you want to present those and reinforce them.

➤ part three RELEVANCE

chapter nine

THE BIBLE'S REVOLUTIONARY PARENTING RULES

SOME OF THE great parents we interviewed have a well-honed intuition that enabled them to make laudable decisions without much effort. Most of the parents, though, really worked hard at Revolutionary Parenting. One of the critical elements they blended into their efforts was studying the Bible to grasp the principles that would lead to success.

How much time have you spent reading, studying, praying about, rereading, and discussing biblical principles for parenting success? Reading books by respected Christian authors can definitely help you gain wisdom for the journey. But there is simply no substitute for the words of God Himself when it comes to making the most of the privilege of raising spiritual champions.

If you have sought scriptural guidance in parenting, you might have been surprised to discover how *little* instruction God gives us in this regard.

I believe there are several reasons for that. First, there is more guidance provided about the nature of spiritual maturity in adults because God knows that parents, in effect, create children in their own image—just as He did with us. We pass on our values and habits, often without realizing the transfer is taking place. Therefore, if He can get adults to adopt appropriate ideals, then they will be likely to incorporate those standards into their parenting efforts. Indeed, few parents would willingly teach their children morals, beliefs, and behaviors that they did not personally embrace as a legitimate foundation for life.

Second, the cultural context of the early church was one in which adults were the class of people focused upon. It was understood during those times that parents took the task of raising children seriously, but their tradition did not foster prolific documentation about children and parenting matters. Those matters would have been discussed between extended family members and close friends. In other words, there were no first-century James Dobsons or Dennis Raineys—no "experts on children and parenting." Parents were expected to turn to God and their spiritual communities to gain the insights and assistance they needed to raise high-caliber devotees of God.

Third, the absence of specific methods of training children is consistent with the Bible. While it is a "guidebook for life," it does not tell us specifically how to do most things, only which matters are significant and what outcomes honor God.

I noticed this truth many years ago in my consulting efforts among churches. The Barna Group has had the privilege of serving thousands of churches around the world, but we recognized that there is no simple set of rules or a one-size-fits-all plan that would guide all churches in all situations. That's simply not how God works. He respects our idiosyncrasies—in fact, He created them—and He appreciates the ever-changing, unique circumstances in which we find ourselves. To make life more exciting and challenging, He gives us room to develop creative biblical solutions to the problems we face.

One of the most intriguing realizations in a biblical study of parenting is how little we're told about how Jesus Christ was raised. You might assume that there are some genuinely mind-boggling parenting lessons we could pick up from seeing what produced the greatest spiritual champion of all time. But God chose not to reveal those matters to us. Perhaps He was afraid that we would try to imitate what Mary and Joseph did, missing the point that what mattered were the character that emerged in Jesus' life and how that was translated into world-changing activity.

Having said all of that, don't assume that the Bible is silent on the topic of parenting. Far from it!

To guide you through the process of identifying critical ideas provided in God's Word on this subject, let me categorize the types of insights you may find most useful as you study the Scriptures that relate to Revolutionary Parenting.

ISSUES IN RAISING CHILDREN

The way we approach children should be influenced by God's thoughts on our young ones. Not only does God give us insights into how to perceive our children and how to interact with them, He is unambiguous in detailing what to make of our offspring.

In the very first book of the Bible, God informs us that children are a gift to us.[1] Just as humans are described as the crowning achievement of His creation, so are children the crowning achievement of our lives, as we partner with God in the miracle of birth. His description of children is that they are a *special* gift—a blessing to the parents and, if the parents do their job well, ultimately a blessing to the world.

Later in Genesis we are instructed that the mere existence of our children is reason to praise God. They may be a gift, and one that demands gobs of attention and energy for many years, but we must not forget that God has shown His love for and trust in us by allowing us to have children. God blesses us through them in various ways.

One example of that blessing is how children draw their mother and father closer together.[2] This is not only through the act of procreation, but through the years of teamwork that the parents jointly venture into while striving to raise spiritual champions. Perhaps more than anything else in life, raising children gives a couple a compelling reason to operate with unity of purpose and process. Early in life, most children stumble onto the practice of dividing and conquering their parents as a means of asserting their own will and getting their way. God's Word reminds us that successful parenting is founded on blending the ideas, skills, and efforts of the parents into a seamless mix of guidance.

Given our children's significance as a special blessing from God, it makes sense that we are instructed never to give up seeking and hoping for our children's well-being.[3] This is certainly where the element of faith in God creeps into our experience. All parents face situations in which they feel overwhelmed, hopeless, ill skilled, or too tired to cope with their circumstances. God's admonition, however, is to realize that we are not alone in parenting these bastions of energy that He has bestowed upon us. Truly the only way we can justify not giving up in some circumstances is to recognize the presence of God and His desire to be our partner in the parenting adventure.

GENERIC GROUND RULES

As parents consider their options, God offers some parameters to shape our parenting capacity.

The first of these ground rules is that it is helpful for us to consider how God has fashioned our own lives.[4] The guidance He has integrated into our development is a model upon which to base the way in which we raise our children. He has disciplined us, and in like manner we are to discipline our children. He has encouraged and rewarded us, and we must do the same with our young ones. In fact, every day He provides us with new parenting lessons and reinforcement of old lessons because we are always *His* children and are always in the midst of being shaped by *Him*. Parenting, then, is a never-ending process of learning more about God, ourselves, and how we can enhance the quality of the lives He has entrusted to us.

Consequently, just as we know that our obedience to God's commands and principles blesses Him, that commitment to obedience also blesses our own children.[5] Not only does such behavior act as a tangible example for our children, but our obedience facilitates God's blessings as we struggle to raise children of light in a culture of darkness.

One of the approaches the Bible encourages us to follow is that of doing whatever we must do to protect the life of our children. We can read about extreme measures taken by Moses' mother (placing the infant in a basket and floating him down the Nile in the hope that his life would be spared) or the anguished cry of a mother to let a prostitute have her child rather than watch King Solomon slice the baby in half.[6] But we must also translate the same principle into less ultimate settings to distance our young ones from danger. Perhaps that means moving to another community to spare our children from gang warfare. Maybe it requires disconnecting the home from cable television to guard the minds and hearts of our young ones.

Whatever the cost, parents are told to spare their children's lives—not just physically, but spiritually, morally, emotionally, and intellectually. That may be why the Scriptures also entreat us to not provoke them to anger or isolation.[7] In the same way that God sought to protect parents from dismay in parenting by commanding children to honor their parents, so does He foster the delivery of that respect by cautioning parents against setting off our young people.

PREPARING KIDS FOR LIFE

God wants parents to prepare their children to lead a godly life. Solomon wrote that transformational parenting produces children who manifest grace and respect while demonstrating a consistent resistance to the lures of sin and evil.[8] These attributes come from the habit of obedience, based upon the instructions and feedback provided by godly parents.[9]

Discipline is one of the keys to Revolutionary Parenting. Scripture notes that God disciplines us because He loves us. The Bible says that such discipline is for our own good.[10] Similarly, if we love our children, one of the most important things we do is discipline them. Such shaping of the minds and hearts of children produces wisdom and grace, and it gives them the will and capacity to resist sin. It gives our children proof of our love for them and their legitimacy as our children. And it brings them the respect of others.[11] The benefits to parents include peace of mind, a happy heart, pride in the child, and hope for their future.[12]

The Bible is clear in suggesting that discipline might include spanking or other forms of reasonable and appropriate physical punishment. There is no excuse for physical abuse or harshness, but the Scriptures do state that "they won't die if you spank them. Physical discipline may well save them from death" (Proverbs 23:13-14).

At the same time, it is expected that parents will empower their children to make good decisions and to live righteously by offering them advice (whether solicited or not), teaching them simple discernment, instilling respect, and helping them to choose their friends.[13] All of these actions are related to parents' responsibility to prepare their young charges for independence and obedience.

A POSITIVE FAMILY ENVIRONMENT

Parenting is not a solitary task; it is to be done in partnership.[14] Not only does the Bible exhort parents to work together as one (hearkening back to the supernatural blending of two lives into one through marriage), but it also states that parents are to be constant role models for their kids.[15] The amount of time spent together, the variety of situations they experience, and the way in which children can grasp the context of their parents' behavior make the mother and father the ultimate living examples of what godliness looks like in real time.

The influence of parental modeling can be clearly seen through the succession of kings that ancient Israel had. References are strewn throughout the Bible identifying bad kings as those who followed the awful example set by their parents and good kings as being those who followed in their parents' hallowed footsteps.[16] You and I may not be royalty in this life, but we have the same impact on the lives of our children as Old Testament kings such as Rehoboam, Jeroboam, and Ahab had on their pampered princes.

The way that parents interact with their children is of great importance to God. The Bible urges us to work at building a relationship with each child—just as God has gone out of His way to do with each of us. The biblical text tells us that the parent-child relationship should be developed on mutual trust and the sharing of important information and experiences. It is through those special moments when intimacies are shared that the bonds of the relationship grow deep.[17]

At the same time, thc rules of family life clearly specify that parents are to have appropriate physical relationships with their children. Nothing can shatter the life of a young person more than being sexually exploited by a trusted family member. Those boundaries are spelled out in no uncertain terms in God's words to us.[18]

Family life is designed to provide children with an environment in which they can grow to maturity at their natural pace of development. To facilitate that outcome, the family is to provide a home that serves as a sanctuary in the midst of the turmoil that accompanies childhood and young adulthood.[19] To make it a truly safe haven, parents are responsible for carrying out their own duties—providing shelter, food, health care, clothing, spiritual experiences, community, and physical safety. When parents fulfill these duties, the children can invest their energy into maturing without the anxieties that so often plague our young people today.

An interesting expectation lodged in the child-rearing passages of the Bible is that parents should also provide their children with some type of inheritance. Often, we think of an inheritance as material wealth: money, housing, or other possessions. The Bible affirms that as a possibility but also underscores an even more important inheritance: the spiritual blessing of the parents.[20] While there is no particular ritual or process described in the Scriptures, it is clear that children treasured this blessing as both a birthright and a spiritual rite of passage that marked one of the significant moments in their lives.

In the course of creating a comforting and nurturing environment, as well as providing their children with valuable resources and relationships, parents also have another task: to nudge their children's development forward by introducing them to the value of hard work. In addition, God expects parents to teach the children obedience to the ways of God and respect for others. These are foundational values that will serve children well as they advance to adulthood.[21]

SHAPING THEIR SPIRITUALITY

The Bible speaks of three ways in which parents are involved in the shaping of their children's spirituality: facilitating understanding, developing character, and advancing their relationship with God.

Facilitating understanding. The simplest but most profound commands given to parents are to read the Bible to their children regularly and to repeat God's commands to them constantly.[22] Exposure to God's Word is irreplaceable in the effort to create spiritual champions: That is the content that shapes young minds and hearts in a meaningful way. There is no substitute for exposure to the Bible. And exposure to the Scriptures must be frequent enough to become a habit. But the exposure must also be reinforced by the parents drawing the crucial lessons and principles from the content, and relating those insights to the child's life.

The Word suggests that there are two ways of accomplishing this application function. First, the stories are to be told in such a way as to develop a healthy faith in God—fearful of His majesty, awestruck by His wisdom and power, bowled over by His compassion and love, and dazzled by His creativity and vision.[23] Second, the exposure to biblical truth should lead to worship and praise.[24] The benefit of reading the Bible is not simply gleaning knowledge that produces personal holiness. The ultimate objective is to generate an urgency to honor God at all times, not only through personal obedience but also through expressions of worship. As parents, we must resist the temptation to follow the cultural path, which emphasizes how the Christian faith benefits "me." Instead, Scripture calls us to turn our focus to God and throw ourselves into glorifying *Him*.

Developing character. We will not have much of a chance of raising spiritual champions, though, if we do not also stress the importance of obedience. This only comes with repetitive training. The Bible admonishes parents to be tireless in their pursuit of purity in their children's lives.[25] From a larger perspective, we might think of this as our effort to develop godly character in our children. Such character, based on the values and morals that are the bedrock of the Bible, naturally lead to appropriate life choices.

The development of Christlike character is naturally linked to the reasons we worship God and fear Him: His sheer holiness and love for us should motivate a desire to live obedient lives. Indeed, the urgency of this quest is perhaps best captured in Paul's first letter to the Thessalonians, in which he reminded them that like a father he "pleaded with . . . encouraged . . . and urged" them to "live your lives in a way that God would consider worthy" (1 Thessalonians 2:12). He captures the sense of absolute necessity to do whatever it takes to foster godly character in our children.

Advancing their relationship with God. All of this is about the relationship that our children develop with God. In that regard, the Bible also encourages us to lead our children to faith through repentance and to confirm that commitment to Christ and a holy lifestyle by getting baptized.[26] Can there be a greater joy in parents' lives than knowing that they contributed in a mighty way to the decision their child has made to be a devoted follower of Christ, and to demonstrate the depth of that commitment through consistently practicing the ways of God?

REASONABLE EXPECTATIONS

One of the most challenging passages God leaves us is in the very beginning of Isaiah, in which the Creator Himself bemoans the fact that "the children I raised and cared for have rebelled against me" (Isaiah 1:2). Could there be a more knowledgeable, capable, loving, forgiving, or righteous parent than the Lord? Yet in this passage He recounts the sting of reality: When people are given the opportunity to make their own choices and live as they see fit, even the most wonderful and wise parent may suffer defeat in the realm of parenting. Even if parents do everything optimally, there are no guarantees that their children will turn out to be spiritual champions.

This dose of objectivity is important for those of us who seek to honor God through the way we raise our progeny. On the one hand, it might help keep us humble (as if most of us need any additional humbling!) and realistic about the parenting enterprise. On the other hand, this passage may also help us lighten up a bit, knowing that we might fail in spite of an outstanding effort because we are working with the same raw material that rejected God: sinful human beings unable to fully restrain themselves when tempted.

CONSISTENCY BETWEEN SCRIPTURE AND SUCCESS

One of the most startling revelations to me after conducting these two forms of research—interviewing spiritual champions and the Revolutionary Parents who raised them, and culling insights from the Bible regarding God's exhortations on Revolutionary Parenting—is the consistency between what each source of information provided! If you list the principles described in the previous chapters of this book, you find that they correspond very closely to the principles and commands in the Bible.

That does not make parenting any easier. We need to enter the parenting world with our eyes open and fully prepared for what we will encounter in the battle for the minds and hearts of our children. Raising a spiritual champion is not a simple job, but God never gives us more than we can handle.[27] He makes sure that we have the ability and the resources to accomplish what we need to accomplish, and causes all of the events and challenges in life to facilitate positive outcomes for His Kingdom.[28] We must persevere with robust faith and remain committed until the end of the tasks we have been given. He will strengthen us and see us through to the end. He has promised that.[29]

But the beauty of this research is that it confirms that if we follow God's principles and commands, He gives us the results He promised. Further, the fact that so many parents have successfully implemented those very ideals suggests that this is a feasible course of action for any parents who are truly committed to God and to their children. The outcomes are not random or accidental: They are predictable and achievable if we are willing to follow the dictates provided by God.

Rapid Review

- Children are God's gift to you. Enjoy and treasure that gift.
- Always look out for your children's well-being. It's your job to protect them.
- In raising your children, work as an inseparable, mutually supportive team with your spouse.
- Remember that your children were made in God's image, not yours; raise them that way.
- We were made to be obedient. Satan lives to undermine those efforts. Do what you can to foster a commitment to doing whatever honors God.

- Discipline your children. It's your job. Nobody else can do it as effectively, nor should you expect them to.
- Provide a positive, nurturing home environment.
- Show your children what Christianity looks like by the way you live.
- Be firm but gentle with them. You want to shape them, not break them.
- Work at helping them to understand the Bible. It's more important than any other book they will ever read.
- Purify their character. It will define them for the rest of their lives.
- Obliterate any obstacles to their relationship with God.

Hands-On

1. Communicate every day with your spouse regarding your parenting. Be sure to clarify where it's going, how it's going, and what needs to be done to pave the way for continuing success in your joint venture.
2. Put together a list of attributes of God's character. Then craft a plan of how you intend to model those same characteristics in your child's life.
3. Consider the different places and activities in which your children are involved each week. Anticipate situations in which they may be at risk, and implement

safeguards and fallback strategies designed to protect them without alarming them.

4. Talk to your children about whether they feel your home is a safe place, a happy environment, and a setting into which they are proud to bring their friends. Hear their comments without being defensive. Do what you can to make their home a compelling sanctuary.

chapter ten

HOW STUDYING REVOLUTIONARY PARENTING CHANGED ME

MY LIFE IS SO FRENETIC at times—more times than I'd like to admit—that it had not occurred to me that if I can do a great job raising my children, the rest of my life is likely to fall into place, if for no other reason than that my priorities will be aligned with God's. But it's true: Several passages of Scripture describe the positive outcome of good parenting as producing peace in the life of the parent.

The notion of having a peaceful heart because of my efficacy as a parent has caused me to reassess all the big plans and dramatic decisions that have characterized my life.

How about you? As you evaluate the state of your life today, do you feel that you have found the groove where your parenting successes have defined your life and enabled you to feel a deeper harmony with the heart of God?

Having spent a couple of years working on this project and truly agonizing over some of the findings, I decided to summarize my own major growth points from the project. I distilled ten personal takeaways that have raised the most serious challenges to my thinking and behavior as a parent.

My life is different from yours, so you may not relate to some of the pressures or challenges pertinent to the Barna household. But the struggle to find a compelling combination of perspectives and practices should resonate with you at some level. In other words, I'm not recommending that you take my ten challenges and adopt them as your own. If anything, they may simply serve as a template for your own reflections and revisions in your parenting strategy.

Toward that end, please consider the value of crafting your own list of lessons learned from the research described, the biblical imperatives revealed, and the reflections about to be shared. Effective growth will only come about as you develop your own insights and plan of action. Perhaps my list will stimulate your thinking.

1. *It doesn't get any more meaningful than this.* When you ponder your life and legacy, what do you think about? My inclination is to focus on grand outcomes—spiritual revolutions, major cultural transformations—along with some of the more fun and frivolous things I want to experience along the way. I recognize that all of this must be undergirded and driven by my faith in Jesus. But for so long, I missed the fact that a spiritual revolution that takes place "out there" is less significant in

God's eyes unless I can facilitate one "in here"—in my own heart, first, and then in the lives of the people who live under the same roof as me. In particular, it is critical that I see such a revolutionizing faith redefine the lives of my children.

Rather than worry about the commute and facilitating operational efficiencies at work, my obsession should be on the spiritual growth curve of each of my kids. Instead of being preoccupied with how my executive team will orchestrate certain deals and deliverables at work, my dominant focus should be on the paths to progress that need to be implemented with my daughters. In other words, my center of gravity has to shift from one base to another. Forget the cultural inertia; this is about being a follower of Christ by adopting and pursuing His objectives.

Like so many parents, I have become adept at critiquing ineffective parenting practices. Perhaps that is a job hazard for a researcher and social critic. But that won't serve as much of a defense before a holy God who has entrusted the precious gift of my daughters' lives into my hands. If I am going to be aggressive about something, it should be in how I intentionally shape the lives of my children.

What about you? Have you come to a place where you can confidently submit that there is nothing more important in your life than how you love and serve God through the way that you raise your children? Are you at peace with the notion that your greatest legacy will be the children who grow up, leave your home, and become the new church body?

2. *To succeed, I have to answer a very fundamental question: Am I making over these children in my image or God's?* My tendency is to do what comes most naturally to me, which is to create an imitation of myself, allowing for some minor differences in personality and physical attributes. But that misses the point, doesn't it? I was made in God's image, not that of my earthly parents. My daughters were not my creation, but His. And if I truly love them I will do what is best for them—which is to shape them in His image, not mine.

   Time to adjust the formula. . . .

   Upon reflection, this makes all the sense in the world. If I want my children to have godly character, then they must be molded into His total likeness: with His values, morals, purpose, goals, beliefs, and attitudes. My own sense of right and wrong must embrace the "true north" perspective; that is, it must reflect what God says, not what I say (until I become sufficiently beholden to God that my life truly reflects His ways).

   As you consider your children, into whose image are you making them? What are the safeguards you have created to protect against merely cloning yourself?

3. *I need to be a better student of God's principles and commands on parenting, since success is based on His standards, not mine.* Maybe this will reduce some of the self-imposed stress

of having the kids live up to my expectations. I've identified and imposed a bunch of expectations that have little to do with God's plan for their lives. It is critical that they be put on the right track. Getting them there is the job my wife and I must accomplish.

To do this, however, I have to be constantly exploring the mind and heart of God to have assurance that I can tell which track is which. Am I studying the Bible often enough and with a purposeful focus? Does my prayer life give God ample opportunity to modify my human inclinations? Are my wife and I on the same page regarding the direction and the details of what this process will look like, and how we will orchestrate our efforts to mold spiritual champions while giving the Holy Spirit ample room to move?

As you examine your own parenting efforts, what is the basis of your choices and actions? How do you translate God's principles and commands into "success" in your children, and what are you doing to increase the chances of producing such outcomes?

4. *Despite a lot of effort and involvement, my parenting has been more reactive than proactive.* I'm very busy. I have a lot of personal goals that I take seriously. But I can serve only one master. This is a crossroads for me: Will I continue to pursue career goals, or will I recognize that career success with parental failure undermines the professional progress made?

There is an obvious right answer for me. This has

dramatic implications for everything I do—and my response to those implications will show just how genuine my claims about wanting to obey God and serve Him fully are. For starters, I will have to do more than just solve problems once they occur and institute retroactive patches on a broken vessel. Instead, it's time to be strategic: to *anticipate* the likely difficulties that will arise and address those pending challenges before they become a reality. It's the old "cut them off at the pass" ploy.

You cannot imagine what havoc this is already reaping with my daily "to do" list. (I'm a chronic list maker. As far as I'm concerned, if it's not on the list, it doesn't exist.) Instead of just foreseeing the potential land mines awaiting me at the office, now the top priority is outthinking my daughters and shifting the assignments and expectations before problems see the light of day.

It has finally occurred to me that so much of what shapes my children's lives is beyond my control that I have to do whatever I can to maximize those elements that are within my control.

I cannot change the kinds of relational experiences they see unfold in television and movies, but I can have a direct influence on whom they embrace as friends and what types of interactions they have with those peers. I cannot determine what direction a favorite television series will take, but I can determine what and how much media my kids will be exposed to. I cannot ensure that the girls will always be well rested and stress free, but I can see to it that they go to bed and wake up at a reasonable time and that they accept new opportunities only if they can handle the impact on their energy, schedule, and emotions.

What did you change today to anticipate what your children will be going through in the coming weeks? Were there any outcomes or discussions related to your children that surprised you? What are the short-term and long-term strategies you are deploying to guide them?

5. *Relational skills are critical—but different ones than I thought.* Most of us believe that we have a good relationship with our kids, even through the dicey high school years. I'm no different. I am confident that my children would feel comfortable telling my wife and me anything that's going on in their lives and that we could reasonably discuss the critical elements of life. Some of the most crucial dimensions of our relationship are in place: We spend time together, are mutually honest, and genuinely care about each other's well-being.

    But the experience of the Revolutionary Parents we researched has stopped me in my tracks. I'm thinking specifically of several dimensions that I have probably fooled myself into thinking I have performed more adequately than I actually have. For instance, I hear what my daughters say, but I don't always listen—that is, deeply process what I hear them saying. The analysis of what my girls tell me doesn't always connect with the core principles of Scripture, enabling me to respond in a way that will shape champions.

    Have you identified what you consider to be the

ten most irreplaceable parenting skills needed to raise spiritual champions? What are you doing to reconfigure your approach and upgrade your capabilities so that you excel in parenting? Between you and your spouse, have you covered the ground necessary to produce children whose lives honor God and advance His Kingdom?

6. *If my children are going to grow spiritually, most of that growth will come from what takes place inside our house.* We are part of a small church that meets in the homes of the families involved. It is a terrific community of faith, and I am grateful for the families that participate. We also have a more peripheral involvement in a more conventional church located in our city. It, too, has some strengths in ministry. The girls also have attended Christian day schools.

Like most parents, I have become uncomfortably comfortable outsourcing the spiritual growth of my children. Sure, we pray together a few times a day and we talk about spiritual matters regularly, but there has been an unconscious reliance upon "them" to teach a lot of the critical biblical content and to provide a variety of experiences designed to lock down their relationship with God and many core principles.

There will never come a time when I can satisfy God by saying, "Look, my church community did a great job of leading my girls to embrace You and Your principles." As we have seen, both the Scriptures and the experience of successful parents show that this is the job of the parents. Not that this is something I'd shy away from—I welcome the privilege—but it does require an intentionality that has not been central on my calendar or in my mind.

As you assess your parenting strategy, how much have you relied upon your church and other spiritual outposts? Does the balance of energy need to shift?

7. *The trajectory of the spiritual war depends on what I—and other parents—do to raise spiritual champions among our children.* From a macroministry perspective, it's actually the little things that count the most. Rather than looking for the big bang that will revolutionize our world, true revolution will come from a series of significant microlevel changes. The little contributions add up to make a big difference.

This has been a stress-relieving revelation for me. Rather than dedicating my life to trying to figure out the great undiscovered evangelistic or discipleship strategy that will draw massive numbers of people to God, the most significant outcome I should move toward is ensuring that my own household is in sync with Him.

That's the beauty of the "body of Christ." If we each pull our own weight, being part of the family of God becomes the ultimate synergistic experience. I don't have to save the world—good thing, because that ain't gonna happen!—but I can make my contribution through the way that my household matures in faith and practice. This has been the way God has worked throughout human history. He has never waited until He had a majority of the people behind Him to introduce a major shift in human reality. He has consistently relied upon the dedication of a remnant of people whose hearts were sold out to His purposes, and He has brought about transformation through those people.

If you (and each Christian family) take small steps forward—as evidenced through the spiritual transformation in our children's lives—then we will live to see a spiritual awakening unlike anything we have witnessed during our lifetime. In your mind, have you accepted the responsibility for changing a small part of the world through your children?

8. *I have to gamble on the long-term gain over the short-term feel-good outcome.* What parent doesn't want to be best friends with his or her children? And the Bible certainly addresses the value of loving your children and having a solid relationship with them. But I have come to realize that rather than being accepted as an adult "best friend" of my children, my most important role is to be a trusted adviser and confidant.

   In some ways this changes everything about my relationship with them. For instance, it guarantees that we will have more conflict and less open sharing. But that may be for the best—for all of us. It also means that there may be delayed gratification in this relationship, as I await the day when my children are sufficiently removed from their childhood and adolescence to understand and appreciate the role I adopted to support them most effectively.

Parenting is full of sacrifices. One of them may be surrendering a natural form of intimacy with your children in favor of a more mature and tutorial form. What is the nature of your relationship with your children? Are you so close that you are one of their gang, or are you willing to create a bit of space and respect in the relationship in order to provide them with the depth of guidance they need?

9. *I am supposed to be a coach—not a benign dictator.* On the one hand, telling kids what to do and expecting them to follow the directions, just because "I'm the parent and I said it's right," doesn't work in a postmodern world. (Postmodernism is one of those contextual factors I do not like but cannot escape.) On the other hand, that style of parenting may never have worked. Scripture suggests that parents are to command their children to do certain things, but that approach is based upon other relational and spiritual pillars being firmly in place. In the end, a coach can set the bar high but cannot make a person satisfy those expectations. All the coach can do is help people understand and prepare them to meet the standards.

   This perspective reminds me that a coach's challenge is to facilitate each person's best performance, blend it with the performance of other team (family) members, and constantly recalibrate what they are doing so that they meet their ultimate goals and achieve what they have defined to be success. In our family, then, I must be crystal clear as to what "success" is all about and guide each family member to embrace that view. Then I must work on developing each child's life to add value to our quest to be the champions God has designed us to be in terms of character and depth of faith.

In practical terms, that means alleviating the pressure on my children to perform in areas that do not meaningfully contribute to their character, social responsibility, and faith. It also means continually relating what the girls are doing to how God sees them and what He expects of them, and helping to shape their mental picture of what they look like when they are successful. Over the years I have pounded home the notion that God birthed each of them to be "a great woman of God"—someone who loves, serves, and obeys Him. As a coach of this God squad, my task is to be relentless in combating the cultural images of "success" with Kingdom imagery and language. That's where the coaching function really kicks in—honing their skills and perspectives to have a compelling mental portrait of a spiritual champion, to be motivated to pursue it, and to believe they can become it.

How's your coaching quotient? You've probably had a number of people coach you throughout your life and help you learn to distill the good practices from the bad. What does your coaching regimen with your children consist of? How do you coach them in tandem with your spouse? When your children think of success in life, what does that mean to them, and how are you aiding them in the quest to be God's little success stories?

10. *Each of my children requires a different, custom-tailored game plan.* This was one of the hardest pills to swallow from this project. Accepting that my kids should strive to own the same principles, beliefs, and character but that they each will need a different plan to get them there took the wind out of my sails for a while. I have always been cognizant of the differences in personality and capabilities of each of my daughters. But conceiving a distinct plan for each of them and becoming comfortable with different types of midcourse corrections, even though we're all on the same flight plan, has taken some getting used to.

    But there is symmetry and beauty in this discovery too. It enables me to rest assured that the wonderful uniqueness of each girl will be cultivated within a proper context of development. It provides my wife and me the opportunity to flex our creative problem-solving and risk-taking skills with greater abandon. And it holds the promise of providing a platform from which each girl can find herself in conjunction with her relationship with God, without having to conform to things that deny her gifts and uniqueness in Christ.

WHAT'S YOUR PLAN OF ACTION?

So now that I have expressed my own trepidations and dreams regarding the next phase of my parenting adventure, I hope you will feel more motivated and confident to do likewise. The parenting insights outlined in this book can be a monumental stepping-stone to a more satisfying parenting experience—and, more important, toward fostering the development of spiritual champions.

As emphasized by both the Scriptures and the Revolutionary Parents, this job is never easy. Given the trajectory of our culture, it's not likely to get any easier. But it is probably the single most important thing you will ever do in your life. May you do it with wisdom and passion for the glory of God, your partner in the process.

INTRODUCTION

1. My previous book was entitled *Revolution*. It describes a growing population of Americans, faith Revolutionaries, who have redefined their spiritual existence; they are not committed to going to church as much as they desire to be the church. Their lifestyles change substantially as a result of that commitment. The numerical growth of that group is poised to radically alter the nation's faith environment by 2025. See *Revolution* (Carol Stream, Ill.: Tyndale House, 2005), or visit http://www.barna.org.

2. Throughout this book I use the term *church* to refer to a Christian community of faith. Whether it is a conventional, brick-and-mortar type of congregation or an alternative form of community such as a house church, a cyberchurch, a marketplace ministry, or some other format, each group is built on committed relationships and designed to facilitate worship, spiritual growth, service, and community. This discussion is expanded in the book I cited above, *Revolution*, and in a series of reports and articles on The Barna Group Web site, located at http://www.barna.org.

CHAPTER 1: A CRISIS IN AMERICAN PARENTING

1. There are an abundance of resources that address these matters. The information mentioned here can be accessed in sources such as the following: U.S. Department of Health and Human Services, *Health, United States, 2005* (Hyattsville, Md.); Annie E. Casey Foundation, *Kids Count* http://www.aecf.org/kidscount; *America's Children in Brief*, http://www.childstats.gov/americaschildren/press_release.asp; U.S. Department of Education, *Fifth Grade* (Washington, D.C., 2006); Thomas D. Snyder, Alexandra G. Tan, and Charlene M. Hoffman, *Digest of Educational Statistics* (Washington, D.C.: National Center for Educational Statistics, 2005).

2. This expectation can be found throughout the Bible as we study God's relationship with people and the commands and principles He gave us for our benefit. Passages such as Deuteronomy 10:12-13 and Luke 10:27-28 get at this expectation. A more complete discussion of this, in the context of developing a biblical worldview, is contained in my book *Think Like Jesus* (Nashville: Integrity Publishers, 2003), 101–117.

3. This survey included interviews with 608 children between the ages of eight and twelve, drawn from across the nation during July 2006. The findings from this and related studies among adolescents by The Barna Group are drawn from a national tracking survey, entitled TweenPoll™, discussed in various reports at http://www

.barna.org.

4. These studies are from the omnibus surveys, part of the YouthPoll™ resource line from The Barna Group. Further results can be found in *Transforming Children into Spiritual Champions* (Ventura, Calif.: Regal Books, 2003); *Real Teens* (Ventura, Calif.: Regal Books, 2002); and at http://www.barna.org.

CHAPTER 2: CONDITIONS FOR REVOLUTIONARY SUCCESS

1. Although we interviewed many parents who raised spiritual champions, we encountered only a few who did so as single parents. Because of the small number of single parents involved in the study, I have chosen not to draw conclusions about the experience of single parents in the child-rearing process. In the future we hope to interview a large enough sample of single parents who have raised extraordinary children to be able to examine them and their experiences more closely.

CHAPTER 4: REVOLUTIONARY PLANNING FOR SPIRITUAL CHAMPIONS

1. These statistics come from our annual nationwide survey of the senior pastors of Protestant churches, known as PastorPoll™. These data come from the study conducted in December 2002.

CHAPTER 5: THE RULES OF REVOLUTIONARY ENGAGEMENT

1. OmniPoll™ W-04, a nationwide survey of 1,004 adults, conducted November 2004 by The Barna Group.

2. TweenPoll™, conducted July 2006 by The Barna Group, among a nationwide random sample of 608 children, ages eight to twelve.

3. Various forms of music were cited by Revolutionary Parents as posing problems, but rap music was by far the most commonly mentioned genre. This is because of the profanity and illegitimate themes more frequently found in rap and the dark or vulgar videos that are typically released by rap artists.

CHAPTER 6: HOW REVOLUTIONARY PARENTS BEHAVE

1. *Baby Busters* is a term used to define the generation born from 1965 through 1983. The phrase was coined in response to the preceding generation, known as the Baby Boomers. After the Boom generation, in which the United States for the first time experienced more than four million new births annually for several consecutive

years, there was a slowdown in the number of births for more than a decade—a "bust" after the "boom."

CHAPTER 7: A REVOLUTIONARY FAITH

1. For more information on the different faith segments in the United States, including insights into non-Christian adults, visit http://www.barna.org and read the free Barna Update reports that describe these groups. Among those reports are "Christians Say They Do Best at Relationships, Worst at Bible Knowledge," June 14, 2005; and "American Faith Is Diverse, As Shown among Five Faith-Based Segments," January 29, 2002.

CHAPTER 9: THE BIBLE'S REVOLUTIONARY PARENTING RULES

1. Genesis 28:3
2. Genesis 29:31-35
3. Luke 9:37-43
4. Deuteronomy 8:5
5. Deuteronomy 28:1-4
6. Exodus 2:1-10; 1 Kings 3:16-28
7. Ephesians 6:4
8. Proverbs 1:8-9
9. Proverbs 6:20
10. Deuteronomy 8:5; Proverbs 1:8; 3:12; 13:1; 19:18; Hebrews 12:7-8
11. Proverbs 1:8-9; 3:12; 29:15; Hebrews 12:7-8
12. Proverbs 3:12; 19:18; 29:15; 29:17; Hebrews 12:9
13. Ruth 2:22; Proverbs 3:21; 23:19-21; 24:21-22; Matthew 15:4; Ephesians 6:3
14. Deuteronomy 21:18-21
15. 1 Kings 9:4; Proverbs 20:7
16. 1 Kings 15:3; 15:26; 22:46; 22:52; 2 Kings 3:1-3
17. Judges 14:16; Ruth 3:5

18. These boundaries appear in different form in several places, but each contains consistent rules. An example is found in Leviticus 18 through 20.

19. Judges 14:19

20. Such blessings and inheritance are addressed in Genesis 27, 48, and 49, as well as in Hebrews 12:17.

21. Ruth 2:2, Ephesians 6:1-3

22. Deuteronomy 6:4-8; 31:11-13

23. Deuteronomy 4:10; Psalm 34:11; Proverbs 24:21

24. Psalm 145:4; Matthew 21:14-16

25. Deuteronomy 6:2; Matthew 18:6

26. Acts 2:38-39

27. 1 Corinthians 10:12-13

28. Romans 8:28

29. 2 Timothy 2:12; Hebrews 10:36; James 1:3-4; 2 Peter 1:5-7; Revelation 3:10

- Barna, George. *Real Teens*. Ventura, Calif.: Regal, 2002.
- ———. *Revolution*. Carol Stream, Ill.: Tyndale, 2005.
- ———. *Think Like Jesus*. Nashville: Integrity Publishers, 2003.
- ———. *Transforming Children into Spiritual Champions*. Ventura, Calif.: Regal, 2003.
- Burns, Jim. *The 10 Building Blocks for a Happy Family*. Ventura, Calif.: Regal, 2003.
- Fowler, Larry. *Rock-Solid Kids*. Ventura, Calif.: Regal, 2004.
- Hagelin, Rebecca. *Home Invasion*. Nashville: Nelson Current, 2005.
- Kimmel, Tim. *Why Christian Kids Rebel*. Nashville: W Publishing, 2004.
- Kinnaman, David. *Teens and the Supernatural*, a report. Ventura, Calif.: The Barna Group, 2006.
- Perkins, Mitali. *Ambassador Families*. Grand Rapids: Brazos Press, 2005.
- Smith, Timothy. *The Danger of Raising Nice Kids*. Downers Grove, Ill.: InterVarsity Press, 2006.
- Stafford, Wess. *Too Small to Ignore*. Colorado Springs: WaterBrook Press, 2005.
- Stecker, Chuck. *Men of Honor, Women of Virtue*. Colorado Springs: Life Journey, 2006.

about the author

GEORGE BARNA has filled executive roles in politics, marketing, advertising, media development, research, and ministry. He founded the Barna Research Group in 1984 (now The Barna Group) and helped it become a leading marketing research firm focused on the intersection of faith and culture. His research has focused on a wide variety of topics, including faith dynamics, leadership, cultural trends, family development, spiritual transformation, and church health.

Since selling a majority share of The Barna Group, he has continued to play a guiding role in the company. He is the principal in Metaformation, a company dedicated to helping people maximize their life journey, and a partner in The Strategenius Group, which provides strategic marketing and business development services.

To date, Barna has written more than 40 books, primarily addressing leadership, social trends, church dynamics, and spiritual development. They include best sellers such as *Revolution*, *Pagan Christianity*, *Transforming Children into Spiritual Champions*, *The Frog in the Kettle*, and *The Power of Vision*. Several of his books have received national awards, and his works have been translated into more than a dozen languages. He serves as the general editor of the BarnaBooks line published through Tyndale. He has had more than 100 articles published in periodicals and regularly writes analyses for *The Barna*

Update, a biweekly research report accessed online (www.barna.org), and a blog on his personal Web site (www.georgebarna.com). His work is frequently cited as an authoritative source by the media. He has been hailed as "the most quoted person in the Christian Church today" and has been named by various media as one of the nation's most influential Christian leaders.

After graduating summa cum laude from Boston College, Barna earned two master's degrees from Rutgers University. At Rutgers, he was awarded the Eagleton Fellowship. He also has a doctorate from Dallas Baptist University. George lives with his wife and three daughters in Southern California. He is a huge fan of the Lakers, the Yankees, great blues guitar playing, pizza, and the beach.